ON PURPOSE
12 Strategies to Reclaim Your Power and Change Your Life

Sarah R. Adams | Veronica Armstrong | Rebecca Barranca | Dr. Erika Brown
Isha Cogborn | Ita Udo-Ema | Tandra Garvin | La'Vista Jones
Pamela D. Smith | Clifford Starks | Connie Vanderzanden

EDITED BY ISHA COGBORN
IN COLLABORATION WITH THE
PLATFORM FOR PURPOSE INCUBATOR

© 2021 Isha Cogborn

All rights reserved. No part of this publication may be reproduced, transmitted or stored in any form or by any means without the written permission of the author except in the case of brief quotations.

The material in this publication is provided for informational purposes only. Procedures, laws and regulations are constantly changing and the examples given are intended to be general guidelines only. This book is sold with the understanding that no one involved in this publication is attempting herein to render professional advice.

For interviews, bulk orders or additional information, contact Isha Cogborn at Isha@EpiphanyInstitute.com.

Published in Chandler, Arizona, USA by Epiphany Institute.
www.EpiphanyInstitute.com

ISBN: 978-1-7332721-1-7
Library of Congress Control Number: 2021908657

Cover design and layout by Riddick Agency
www.RiddickAgency.com

This book is dedicated to my son, Deon.

Keep working to figure it out. That's often the hardest part.

Table Of Contents

	Introduction	6

Part I - Your Life

Chapter 1	**Tandra Garvin**		10
	Eight Habits to Your Next Level Life		
Chapter 2	**Pamela D. Smith**		24
	Designing an Intentional Life		
Chapter 3	**Isha Cogborn**		34
	How to Fight Fear and Build Authentic Confidence		
Chapter 4	**Veronica Armstrong**		51
	Seven Ingredients to a Secret Sauce: Leave Behind Limiting Beliefs to Embrace a Mindset of Success		
Chapter 5	**Clifford Starks**		62
	How to Bounce Back from Setbacks		
Chapter 6	**La'Vista Jones**		72
	Reconnect with Your Joy Through Self-Care		
Chapter 7	**Rebecca Barranca**		82
	Ten Ways to Live a More Natural Life Everyday		

Part II - Your Business

Chapter 8	**Dr. Erika Brown**		96
	Breaking Patterns of Chaos that Stifle Your Productivity		
Chapter 9	**Connie Vanderzanden**		112
	Your Best Team Member: Money		
Chapter 10	**Isha Cogborn**		124
	Platform for Purpose: How to Grow Your Audience and Your Impact		
Chapter 11	**Ita Udo-Ema**		136
	Harnessing the Power of Storytelling		
Chapter 12	**Sarah R. Adams**		152
	The Importance of Being You		
	Isha Cogborn		160
	Final Thoughts		
	Notes		162

ON PURPOSE / **12** Strategies to Reclaim Your Power and Change Your Life

Introduction

by Isha Cogborn

Life isn't fair.

I remember hearing that phrase early and often during my childhood as I protested not having nice playground equipment like the school across town or having to dress up like an old lady in a school play instead of getting to wear cute leotards like the other girls because my teacher thought I was too fat.

It wasn't fair to me when teachers and administrators in my high school made certain students aware of scholarships or opportunities to attend summer enrichment programs but not others. This was critical, because back then there was no internet to democratize the flow of information.

I knew it wasn't fair to be routinely followed around in stores because an associate thought I might shoplift or having young suitors afraid to cross Eight Mile Road to visit me because their fathers and uncles warned them about the dangers of "driving while Black" in certain communities. When I talked to my classmates about my experiences, many insisted that

I was overreacting or imagining the biased treatment. Now that we live in a world where bystanders are able to share injustices they witness through the lens of their camera phone, many people who were once insulated from these events are forced to acknowledge them.

The lesson I learned as a child still stands today — life *isn't* fair. Has that reality kept you from pursuing what you truly desire? If so, you're in the right place. This book is all about reclaiming your power to create the life you really want.

Maybe you're still working through the trauma of your childhood or have been given a serious medical diagnosis. If you're like me, you may feel like the way your brain is wired frequently leads to actions that sabotage your success. Perhaps it feels like you have to overcome obstacles in your business or career that your peers don't have to deal with. Or maybe you're so beaten down by fatigue, burnout and setbacks that you feel like throwing in the towel and accepting whatever life you end up with.

Even if it feels like the deck is stacked against you, please don't give up. When you tap into the power of purpose, coupled with practical strategies and the support of a person or two who believe in you, you'll be blown away by what you can accomplish.

The twelve chapters you're holding provide practical strategies and tactics to help you successfully work through many of the challenges standing in your way — even if you didn't create them.

This book is divided into two sections — Your Life and Your Business. Whether you're traditionally employed, own a business, are a stay-at-home parent, retired, or are outside of the job market for any other reason, you'll find a wealth of helpful strategies in Part I. While Part II contains nuggets that can be useful to everyone, they're especially focused on entrepreneurs. At the end of each chapter, you'll also find an exercise designed to help you put the principles from the author into practice. If you don't want to write in your book, you can visit **PlatformForPurposeBook.com** enter code **READER** to download the supplemental content.

Finally, we'd love to hear from you! I encourage you to connect with the authors to share how their strategies helped you. As you read, feel free to skip around to find what you need right now based on where you are in your personal development journey.

This book is a collaboration from members of the **Platform for Purpose Incubator**. If you're an expert or thought leader and would like to be a part of future projects like this, visit **PlatformforPurpose.com** to learn more.

Happy Reading!

Isha Cogborn, Editor

ON PURPOSE / **12** Strategies to Reclaim Your Power and Change Your Life

Part I
Your Life

ON PURPOSE / 12 Strategies to Reclaim Your Power and Change Your Life

Learn About
Tandra Garvin

Tandra Garvin is the owner of Golden Trinity Health Care and an entrepreneur at heart. Tandra is fully involved in all aspects of her patient care with over twelve years of experience. Her work spans the health care spectrum from bedside to mentoring. Tandra's primary methodology and approach to health care is to provide increased levels of preventative care and wellness education to better the lives of her patients. Mind, body and soul are her passions and provide the foundation for the care she gives to all.

Tandra is also a nurse leader focused on educating and supporting nursing students through internships, providing feedback, and sharing her experience. One of her goals is to equip nurses with the knowledge and skills necessary to practice with confidence and provide quality care. She also uses her expertise to help other small businesses provide care to patients.

Connect with Tandra Garvin
Email: tgarvin@goldentrinityhealthcare.com

Chapter One
Eight Habits to Your Next Level Life

by Tandra Garvin

When I was young, I often sat on the back porch and daydreamed about a better future. As I let my imagination soar, I was magically transported out of the projects and poverty, picturing the lovely home I'd live in one day with a real backyard. I dreamed of traveling the world, something that couldn't be paid for with food stamps. My family told me to keep dreaming, but it usually felt like a mockery of my desires.

This life, while full of love and security from the relatives who chose to take care of me, just wasn't enough. I knew there had to be more. Not because I saw other people living it, but because the dream down on the inside of me felt too real. And if it was real, I knew I could figure out how to get there.

Learning to Live Unlimited
Nevertheless, as the years progressed and life piled on, the dream became more and more distant. After being raised by my grandmother and aunt, I went to live with my mother at the age of eight where I

watched her suffer years of abuse at the hands of my stepfather. My siblings and I also become the target of his rage at times. By the time I was sixteen, I'd had enough and moved out, living "pillar to post" as I bounced back and forth between friends.

Like my mother, I got pregnant with my first child as a teenager. By the time I was twenty-two, I had two kids, was on welfare, and was living in the same projects where I had once sat on the back porch and dreamed of a better life.

I married the father of my second child and had another baby. I often overheard relatives saying that I wouldn't accomplish anything in life outside of having a bunch of kids. My self-esteem was shattered.

I remembered how when I was young, I wanted things that my family couldn't afford. I didn't want that for my children, so I worked all the hours I could so my children wouldn't suffer the same fate. When I got divorced and instantly had to adjust to life as a single mother again, the stakes felt even higher. Later, my children told me they really didn't care about the "stuff"— they just wished I had been home more.

After my failed marriage, I resolved that I would never make the trip down the aisle again. In fact, it was something that Kevin, my divorced buddy from work, and I both agreed on. I admired how smart and professional Kevin was. Hanging around him made me want more for myself.

That's when I decided to enroll in nursing school. When I shared the news with my family, they told me I couldn't do it while raising three children. But Kevin told me I could do anything I wanted to do if I worked at it, and that he would help me.

He was right. With Kevin as my biggest cheerleader, I graduated nursing school, passed the boards, and added the letters RN to my name. Not only that, but my buddy Kevin also gave me a new last name. So much for never getting married again!

Becoming a registered nurse wasn't easy. The late nights and early mornings had me on the verge of quitting more than once, but I stayed committed. I began to see the dreams I had as a child coming true before my eyes. We bought a nice house with a backyard. We even began to travel the world. While at times I had thrown away the vision, God had not.

After twelve years of working as an RN in the Intensive Care Unit of a hospital, I felt like I was still capable of more. So, I went back to school, earned a master's degree and became a nurse practitioner. It was a challenging four-year journey, and I wanted to quit every day. But as I look back now, I am so glad I didn't.

During the journey, my husband Kevin was diagnosed with lung cancer. When he got the diagnosis, I thought I should just quit school and pick it up later, but the Holy Spirit told me: Baby girl, I got you. My husband was also against me quitting.

I also decided to pursue a Psychiatric Mental Health Nurse Practitioner degree, giving me the unique qualification to treat those dealing with depression, PTSD, anxiety, and many other mental health conditions, while also focusing on their physical health.

I completed the program and passed my boards on the first attempt. But after working as a nurse practitioner for another company for a year, I had an epiphany. I discovered how much revenue I was generating for my company, while my entire salary went towards paying taxes based on the combined income generated by me and my husband.

That motivated me to start my own company, Golden Trinity Healthcare. This gave me the ability to save more money on taxes while having more influence over how I served the community.

My story is one of learning how to live limitlessly. I had to learn how not to limit myself based on others' negative comments or doubts. I also had to learn not to limit myself based on my own failures and regrets. And I learned how to push through obstacles instead of letting them block me from my goals.

What about you? Can you relate to my story? Maybe others are discouraging you or doubting your ability to reach your goals. Do you have regrets about past decisions or events? Are obstacles impeding you? Maybe the way forward to something better looks impossible.

The key word for me is *learned*. If I learned to live limitlessly, you can too.

I learned that to reach the next level, there are eight habits we need to develop. Let me walk you through them.

TANDRA'S PRESCRIPTION TO BUILDING
YOUR BEST LIFE

1. **Be the Author of Your Story**
   Too many of us base our lives on what others expect from us, whether those expectations are great or limited. What would it look like if you took back the pen and decided to write your own story? It doesn't matter if others don't think you're capable or that you've made a lot of mistakes. What matters is what you believe about yourself and what you're willing to do about it.

2. **Invest in Yourself**
   I broke my back working to give my kids anything they wanted without thinking twice about it. But my life was transformed when I became willing to invest that same time, energy, and money into my dreams. Never stop learning and don't wait for your employers to invest in you. Attend conferences. Keep reading and studying. Get a mentor. Stop telling yourself you don't have the time or money to develop yourself. You may not have the ability to do everything you want to do, but you can do something. So do it. Unapologetically.

3. **Don't Be Afraid to Do Hard Things**
   Even though He can, don't expect God to set everything in your lap and make it easy. God is going to let you do what you can, and He will step in and do what you cannot do.

   While I was in school, I could have found a million reasons to quit, but I'm glad I didn't. I see many students stop going to school because of issues with finances, family illness, or just doubts about their abilities. I could have checked all of those boxes. In addition, I was a single mother of three small kids, working full-time to support my household while going to school. Several of my family members thought I was wasting my time. They said I should focus on raising my kids and worry about going to school when they were older. What if I had listened to them? I would not be living my best life, doing what I absolutely love!

> **The key word for me is learned. If I learned to live limitlessly, you can too.**

While I was taking my prerequisites, I was used to getting straight A's. When I took my first nursing school exam, I made a D and you would have thought someone told me the sky was falling. I cried and rehearsed quitting in my head several times. It took one optimistic classmate to touch me on the shoulder and say, "We are going to get through this together." Finding that encouraging tribe in nursing school was very beneficial.

Obstacles will arise; just know that the finish line is ahead. When you fail, get up, dust yourself off, and keep going.

4. **Turn Self-Pity to Busyness**
   If you dislike your job because they don't pay you enough, don't appreciate you, or don't give you the opportunities you deserve, what are you going to do about it? I started my own business

because I did not want my employers to dictate my schedule by telling me I had to work weekends or holidays.

Now, let's be clear—I'm not telling you to quit your job. In some cases, you can get what you want through negotiation. Don't be upset because the new employee started at $50 per hour but you make $35. What did you negotiate? Can you make yourself more valuable through certifications or specialization?

5. **Let Go of Bitterness and Make Yourself Better**
Release any bitterness you may be holding on to because people may have counted you out in the past. Some people can't see a great future for you because they don't see a great future for themselves. That's on them.

   Learn to see yourself the way God sees you and know that if He put the dream in your heart, it's possible.

6. **Don't Be an Imposter**
I remember when I first became a nurse practitioner, I was so impressed with my instructor that I started buying clothes to look like her and even doing my hair like her. One day I sensed God telling me not to be an imposter. I sensed Him telling me, Tandra, I created you to be you. You will have more success and fulfillment by being yourself.

   Thank God for that revelation. I was set free to be Tandra Garvin — the nurse practitioner with the funny voice who likes to wear sequins. Can you imagine falling into the imposter trap and finding out that the person you were trying to model was an imposter? We'd end up living in a world full of imposters. That is not God's plan!

7. **Know When It's Time to Go**
   A key takeaway I have learned during my career is not to become complacent. When I noticed that I was getting bored or work became mundane, that was always a tell-tale sign to level up.

   If you have a dream and do not know where to start, I encourage you to meditate on it and seek God regarding the process. God often will use people to speak into your life as well. Getting a coach is helpful with developing a plan in place to execute your vision. I used to say, "I am not paying someone to tell me what I know I need to be doing." I kindly eat those words now.

8. **Pay It Forward**
   As you begin to make strides, it's important to be willing to teach others. Be the kind face and provide encouraging words to others who don't have it all figured out yet. Remember, someone helped you!

   When it comes to financial goals, it can feel like you're being a humble and godly person not to desire much. But if you're just getting by financially, how can you help others? I remember the days of not having enough or feeling like my dreams were out of reach because of money. It feels amazing to be able to financially support people and causes that I care about. But that wouldn't be the case if I had settled. Thoughts and prayers are good, but it's nice to be able to send a check along with the prayers.

I love my story now. I love that my journey includes helping people from all backgrounds do what I did — break through limited expectations and excuses to go after what they really want in life, even if it doesn't seem possible.

As I look back, I realize my primary motivation didn't come from trying to prove others wrong, but instead, to prove myself right. I do enjoy hearing others who told me I wouldn't succeed now tell me how proud they are of me. But I had to find the motivation within me.

One of the most rewarding parts of my success is being able to help others through the work I do and from the financial freedom my six-figure business provides.

I also love the freedom that comes with entrepreneurship. I get to decide how much and how often I work. This is the first time in my life that I don't have to punch a time clock!

What is God showing you or telling you that seems impossible today? Don't ignore it. Invest the energy and resources into figuring out how to make it your reality.

As you see from my story, the path will not always be easy, but don't take that as a sign that you're on the wrong path or that you're not capable of more. Be willing to work through frustration, fear, and even disappointment. Get help. Build a strong support system and be sure to take care of yourself physically, mentally, and spiritually in the process.

I can almost guarantee you that there will be times you will want to quit. But let me tell you, if I knew it was going to be this good on the other side, quitting wouldn't have even crossed my mind. You can do this—I'm living proof.

PUT IT INTO PRACTICE
Limitless Living Art Project

Just like art, daring to execute your vision for your life and legacy can be daunting. There are endless, nagging what-ifs that paralyze us:

> *What if we place the pen on the page and make a flaw?*
> *What if all of our efforts come to nothing?*
> *What if instead of a work of art, we create a flop that proves our every insecurity to be true?*

My friend, it's time to disarm our what-ifs by anticipating the fruit that comes with persistent effort and resilient hope.

Just as I shared earlier, as a child I dreamed of what life would look like if I were operating at my best. And now, I invite you to do the same. Grab a piece of paper and draw (or craft using magazine clippings and cutouts) the picture of what a "you" operating without limits looks like.

Some questions to consider:
- What fulfilling roles does your unlimited self play?
- What challenges does your best self overcome?
- What investments does the courageous you make in yourself?
- How does this generous version of yourself pour into others?

Download exercise from the "Resources for Readers" section, password "Reader" at PlatformforPurposeBook.com.

Learn About Pamela D. Smith

Pamela D. Smith is a certified life coach who empowers women to grow into their next desired level. She knows what it's like to feel stuck and wants to help her clients go from enduring life to enjoying life.

A certified coach with the John Maxwell Team, Pam is also an award-winning performer and trainer in the airline industry and author of the books, Harvesting Your Pearls and Becoming a Better You by Unleashing Your Greatness. She is passionate about personal growth and with her support, clients are experiencing results in months that others take years to accomplish on their own.

With a lifelong passion of encouraging and helping others, Pam is an avid volunteer, supporting both domestic and international causes, including serving as a small group leader focused on personal growth at Faith Christian Center in Phoenix, Arizona.

In her free time, she enjoys traveling and spending time with the loves of her life: Her husband, children, and grandchildren.

Connect with Pamela D. Smith

Website: PamHasFavor.com
Email: Pam@PamHasFavor.com

Chapter Two
Designing an Intentional Life

by Pamela D. Smith

How often do we pay attention to the daily, often mundane details in our lives?

Take a quick moment, about 30 seconds or so, and let's replay this morning's routine. Can you remember what you did? Maybe you woke up, brushed your teeth, had coffee, took some time for devotion, and then exercised. What happened next? Did you drive to work or scoot over to your work from home spot? Do you even recall those steps happening, or were they a blur? Scientific studies show, most of us live 95% to 97% of our lives on autopilot. We don't consciously think about many of the things we are doing each day. Are you surprised by this high percentage and can you relate? I was and I can.

We are creatures of habit and if not careful, it can lead us to mindlessly engaging in the same tasks and behaviors every day. By definition, using the word routine as an adjective literally means that something is performed as a "regular procedure" rather than for a special reason. If that doesn't describe what most of us do on a daily basis, I don't know what does! How many times have we planned to run an errand, but can't remember the traffic signs or landmarks? Better yet, we arrive at our destination and can't even remember turning in to park.

Friends, we have to be intentional about what we are doing and where we are going. Our lives simply cannot be left on autopilot.

As we journey toward intentional living, I want to give you some practical steps to teach you how to be purposeful about your personal growth journey. We'll refer to them as "Pam's Pearls". Together, we'll rediscover the benefits of being intentional in our personal growth and I'll leave you with my 4-step framework for producing more focused efforts toward your growth. Ready? Great! But before we begin, let's make sure we're all on the same page and have a common understanding of how being intentional is defined going forward.

WHAT DOES IT MEAN TO BE INTENTIONAL?

When we are intentional, we are determined in word and action, resulting in more meaningful and fulfilling lives. It means we make thoughtful, not haphazard choices in our lives. We actively interact and engage with our lives regularly and consistently. Exercising intentionality empowers us to live in alignment with our purpose, because we strategically implement habits and take focused action to achieve our goals. You have to know where you want to go in order to take action every day.

Living intentionally is not always easy to do. We often get caught up with the thoughts in our head and wrapped up in the daily grind of moving from one thing to the next. It's very easy to lose sight of what we are working towards. How many people actually have a vision for their lives or a goal they are actively working towards? Setting a daily intention of being the best version of ourselves with what we've been given is certainly a great place to start.

When we talk about action-focused intentionality, we can create a mental picture of it as if we were building our

Designing an Intentional Life

dream home from the ground up. Allow me to share my 4-step framework (Pam's Pearls) using this metaphor for a practical and intentional outline to create our personal growth journeys.

As you build a home you need certain things. You need a location, a sturdy foundation, a blueprint, and then you execute your build. Let's dig a little deeper into each of these steps.

Pam's Pearl #1: Scout Your Desired Location

When building a house, we must first decide on the right location. This will include answering questions on whether or not we'd want to live in a gated community with or without a pool, or whether we'd want to live close to our jobs or church. Maybe it would be nice to have a view of the mountains or the water. Additionally, is there a particular draw to building downtown where there is access to entertainment? Or, if we have children, is this area in a family-oriented community with good school districts and libraries? There are so many variables! Location is super important. We must set and determine our desired location.

In the same way, we must intentionally set and focus on a desired location for our personal growth journey. Our location is simply the area or areas in which we want to improve. That location may look like a promotion or a desire to lose weight, or to get married. Whatever that is, we must choose.

Tip: Start small. Select one area — maybe two — on which to focus. Overwhelm is real and can be a stumbling block to reaching our goals.

Pam's Pearl #2: Establish a Secure Foundation

Now that we've decided on our location, the next step is establishing a sturdy foundation. Most foundations are constructed with cement or concrete, because the foundation of your home must be strong and reliable.

Foundations are the literal bedrocks of our homes to keep them stable. They also take time to cure and set. Friends, we can't rush this process, or else the foundation will not be able to withstand the weight of the home. Also, when a storm comes or a strong wind blows through, a properly set and solid foundation will keep our houses from being destroyed.

What is our sturdy foundation in our personal growth journey? Knowing our "why". Our why gives us a benchmark to build upon that won't be shaken with every passing idea, fleeting relationship, or transient opportunity. Just like a physical foundation will help our home weather storms and wind, a foundation that is based on our why will help us focus and navigate the inevitable storms that life will bring. Life's storms show up in the form of obstacles, barriers, and limiting beliefs. This may even manifest in a way we've never experienced before, making us momentarily feel shaky and unsteady. But here's the thing: they won't destroy you, because the intentional, sturdy foundation we've established will allow us to quickly get back on our path.

Pam's Pearl #3: Draft a Blueprint
After we've selected our location and established a secure foundation, what's next? Great question! Now, we draft a blueprint. What do we want our dream home to look like? How many rooms and windows? Where should the kitchen be and how big is our home going to be overall? Of course, we can't forget to include the supplies we will need. Last, but certainly not least, we have to know what it will cost us. A proper blueprint will give us an exact outline of where, what, who, why, and how much.

A proper blueprint for our personal growth will do the same as one for a house. What are our resources and how do we identify or categorize them? Human, financial, spiritual, etc.? Do we have an idea what the outline of our goal(s) looks like? What materials will we need to build it out? Most importantly, we have to draft a blueprint for intentional personal growth so we can clearly see what it will cost us. Building a house has a specific cost, and so does intentionally showing up for ourselves every day. Every yes is a no to something or someone else, and vice versa. It may cost us our time, money, or intangible resources. The cost may be minimal or very expensive, but we will never know unless we actually get our blueprint laid out. To live intentionally, it helps to have a vision or in this case, a blueprint for your life. That vision will help you to align your behavior with your ambitions.

Pam's Pearl #4: Execute Your Build

Our final step brings the first three together. We have done the work of acquiring our desired location, establishing a secure foundation, and drafting our blueprint. We are now ready to execute our build! This is what we've planned and waited for! Here

> **Once I committed myself to bringing that vision to fruition, I started living each day in a way that aligned with my goal.**

is where we finally see our dream home come to life. We get to use all our resources identified in our blueprint in a creative, yet functional and fulfilling way. After this labor of love is complete, our dream home is ready to enjoy.

How does this translate into our action plan for our personal growth journey? Doing the work. We engage in the tasks and behaviors that lead us closer to our goal every single day. Some of us may have large financial goals like reaching a certain income or getting out of debt. Both are equally important.

You may have unique health goals requiring specific training or maybe you just want to lose a few pounds. Both require action. This is where our intentionality is put to the test. Are we ready?

I believe there is one question we should ask ourselves every day. We discussed it above in the section about our foundations. That question is, "What is my why?" There is something truly beneficial about identifying and writing our intentions on paper that can keep us accountable while working towards a life lived with intention. I once heard someone say that we should take actions today that our future selves would appreciate. It encouraged me to take some time to intentionally reflect on what I wanted my life to look like in the future. This really resonated with me, and I hope it will for you as well.

Here's how I experienced living life with intention: Years ago, I had a vision of losing 40 pounds. I was overweight and uncomfortable with the person I saw in the mirror. Once I committed myself to bringing that vision to fruition, I started living each day in a way that aligned with my goal. I stopped eating certain foods and followed a strict workout regimen. It was difficult at first, but I was determined to stick to it. I was determined to make my dream a reality. I wanted to be healthy — that was my "why". After a year of remaining committed to my goal, my vision was fulfilled.

Friends, it's been eleven years since I accomplished that goal for myself. I've kept the weight off and people can hardly believe I was ever that size. Sometimes committing to a vision means committing to a lifestyle change. When I decided on the goal of being 40 pounds lighter, I unknowingly committed myself to maintaining a healthier lifestyle. Since then, my diet and fitness have changed in ways I would have never imagined.

Today, I find myself in the early stages of a new vision. I am on a journey to be more grounded and fulfilled.

And this will involve focusing on my coaching goals, my relationships, and myself.

Life is a perpetual journey; it doesn't stop once you reach one goal. It's a continuous process. Since life is ongoing, expect your journey to be unending as well. The beauty of this framework is that after using it to achieve one goal, you can recycle these four steps to achieve another. It's the act of working towards a vision or a goal that can make it worthwhile.

PUT IT INTO PRACTICE
What's Your Vision?

Maybe you've experienced great success, passively going through life, and you've finally realized that same behavior won't get you to the next level. That passive way of just allowing things to happen in your career—in your life—can no longer be your norm. Perhaps, it's been the exact opposite. Maybe you've been in a rut, just waiting for your life to change, and you've finally been awakened to the calling on your life, and you know it's time to step out.

We must INTENTIONALLY SEEK and CREATE opportunities with a vengeance. We must INTENTIONALLY speak truth over our lives! No matter your history, you can change your future! It's time to make that move. It's time to take that step. It's time to get INTENTIONAL with our living... and do all that we've been called to do!

From Mindless to Intentional: 3 Moments to Exercise Intentionality

1. Avoid MINDLESSLY surfing social media on your smartphone, and INTENTIONALLY use moments of boredom to strengthen a healthy habit, reach a personal goal, or build connection with others.

    A few suggestions:

    - Take a moment to appreciate the beauty of nature.
    - Watch a training that will sharpen your mindset or skillset.
    - Check-in on a loved one.

2. Minimize your time spent MINDLESSLY (and passively) racking up screen time, and become more INTENTIONAL about adding more physical activity into your daily routine.

A few suggestions:

- Use an app to set an active timer throughout your day.
- Alternate between sitting and standing as you work or watch entertainment.
- Commit to a weekly self-assessment of your screen time. (Most smartphones help you manage this with an end-of-week report.)

3. Before MINDLESSLY saying "yes" to a request, reflect INTENTIONALLY about whether it would be a great use of your time, energy, and resources.

A few suggestions:

- Track your progress toward your goals so that you're aware of how incurring another obligation may help or hinder your success.
- Curve out non-negotiable time to attend to your priorities, as well as to rest and recover.
- Establish boundaries with others that help you make commitments from a place of good emotional health.

Download exercise from the "Resources for Readers" section, password "Reader" at PlatformforPurposeBook.com.

Learn About
Isha Cogborn

Isha Cogborn is the founder of Epiphany Institute, where she helps people connect their purpose and passion to their profession.

As a nationally sought-ought speaker, three-time author and podcast host, Isha couples two decades of experience helping corporations and individuals make a greater impact with the resilience birthed from being a teenage mother on welfare, corporate layoffs and a bout with homelessness after a failed business venture. In 2017, Isha also founded Startup Life Support to help entrepreneurs overcome the fear, overwhelm and isolation of starting a business.

Isha earned a degree in Broadcast & Cinematic Arts from Central Michigan University and is member of Alpha Kappa Alpha Sorority, Inc. The Michigan native now lives in the Phoenix area, where she enjoys Netflix binges and Peloton rides.

Connect with Isha Cogborn:
Website: EpiphanyInstitute.com
Email: Isha@EpiphanyInstitute.com

Chapter Three
How To Fight Fear And Build Authentic Confidence

by Isha Cogborn

Maggie's Missing Piece of the Puzzle
Maggie had been dreaming of becoming a published author since she was a little girl. As she sat in rush hour traffic on her daily commute, ideas that she wanted to put on paper effortlessly floated through her head. Maggie made a commitment to herself to finally make writing a priority, scheduling non-negotiable, uninterrupted time every weekend. The more she wrote, the more excited she got about how many people she'd help with the knowledge she would be sharing.

On her weekly visit to the hair salon, she told her stylist, Alicia, that she had finally gotten serious about writing, but she worried that it would all be for nothing because she didn't know the first thing about how to actually put a book into the world. Alicia told Maggie that she had another client who coached people through the process of getting their books self-published, including everything from editing to layout and cover design. She knew several people who had been pleased with her work, and she encouraged her to schedule a consultation.

Maggie floated out of the salon on cloud nine, excited that all of the pieces were finally coming together. But she never called the book coach. In fact, she stopped writing altogether.

Alicia's Big Opportunity
That same week, Alicia, the hair stylist, invited her best friend Michael over for Sunday brunch. She couldn't wait to tell him that after nearly two years and thousands of dollars invested in development, she was finally ready to launch her own line of hair care products. She even had a chain of salons owned by her mentor ready to place a huge order with a commitment to keep her products on the shelf! All she had to do was decide on her pricing structure for bulk sales and send the proposal.

That week, Alicia spent every free moment online looking at her competitors. After reviewing dozens of other products, she started to question everything. Did her labels look cheap? Why would people buy her products when there were more established brands that were much less expensive? What if she got bad reviews online? She felt paralyzed. Michael tried to get her to just send in the proposal, but after weeks of ignoring requests from her mentor to follow through, she lost the deal.

Michael's Dream Job
When Alicia's friend Michael got to work on Monday, his manager popped into his office to tell him that he should take a look at a job that had just been posted in another department. It wasn't that she was trying to push Michael out, but he had been a top performer in his current role for years, and she just didn't have the budget to pay him what he deserved.

This role was a significant promotion with greater responsibility, visibility with the C-suite leaders of their Fortune 100 corporation, and a big fat raise. His duties would also include becoming a spokesperson for the company, speaking at conferences around the country and occasional media appearances.

Michael felt like someone had just placed his dream job in front of him! He had been growing increasingly frustrated that his talents were being underutilized and was on the verge of looking for opportunities outside of the company. He read the job description over and over again and began to picture himself functioning in his new role.

A week after the deadline for internal applicants closed, his manager followed up to ask if HR had reached out yet about his status. His gaze shifted to the floor, and he told her that he decided not to apply. His manager did her best to hide her frustration and disappointment as she closed Michael's office door and walked away.

The Real Problem
With wonderful opportunities within their reach, why did Maggie, Alicia, and Michael blow it?

Maggie might tell you that she couldn't afford to hire the book coach, although she got her hair done weekly and was on a first-name basis with the Amazon delivery guy. She never even bothered to find out how much it would cost! Alicia would probably say she was just trying to gather enough information to make the best decisions for her business. Michael would firmly state that with so much uncertainly in the economy, the safest move was to stay in his current role. You know how the saying goes—last hired, first fired.

But all three are dealing with the same issue—they let fear bully them out of what they really wanted.

Can you relate? Fear doesn't always show up as knocking knees, sweaty palms, and heart palpitations. In fact, it's often cleverly disguised as procrastination, fatigue, and analysis paralysis.

Want to know one of the best antidotes for fear? Authentic self-confidence.

Defining Self-Confidence

Dictionary.com defines self-confidence as, "a feeling of trust in one's abilities, qualities and judgment." Your level of self-confidence can be influenced by a number of factors, such as your culture, upbringing, religious beliefs and life experiences. If you can recite the Bible scripture Romans 12:3 by heart, which admonishes to not think of yourself more highly than you ought, having a healthy degree of self-confidence may literally feel like a sin.

You can't blame yourself for being a product of your environment. But once you become aware of these limiting beliefs, you have a responsibility to yourself to make the adjustment.

What Does Self-Confidence Look Like?

Self-confidence serves as a magnifier of our thoughts. If you know that you add significant value to the company you work for, a high degree of self-confidence leads you to ask for a raise with evidence to support why you deserve it. A low degree of self-confidence translates into waiting for your boss to decide to give you one.

> **Want to know one of the best antidotes for fear? Authentic self-confidence.**

How does low self-confidence show up?

- Not speaking up when you have a suggestion or question.
- Deferring to others even when you have a strong urge that you're right.
- Not pursuing opportunities that you're interested in.
- Unwillingness to take risks.

- Not asking for the sale.
- Low-balling yourself in salary negotiations and pricing.
- Extreme over-preparation and perfectionism.
- Declining opportunities that put you in the spotlight.
- Unhealthy comparison.

What Is Low Self-Confidence Costing You?

A 2008 study by the University of Messina shows that individuals from blue-collar families who possess higher levels of self-confidence earn roughly $7,000 more per year than their peers who have low self-confidence. In white-collar classes, the gap is even larger. Those with high self-confidence earn approximately $28,000 more annually than those who lack confidence. Over a 40-year career, that adds up to as much as $280,000 to $1.12 million in lost earnings (*Drago*).

Low self-confidence can also lead to lower levels of entrepreneurial activity. How many people do you know with great business ideas who talk about it, but never move forward? You may have called them (or yourself) lazy or unfocused, but it's likely that they're just scared. People with higher levels of self-confidence are more likely to take risks, start their own ventures, and enjoy the fruits of their labor.

Can You Build Self-Confidence?

What do you do if you weren't born with self-confidence oozing through your veins? Or if past experiences drained the confidence that you once possessed? Do you just chalk it up as your fate? That other people are simply destined to have greater success because they're wired differently?

Much like a muscle, self-confidence can be developed over time. Just like you don't do ten reps with a 5-pound weight and expect to be ready for a bodybuilding competition, don't expect to simply recite a few positive affirmations and turn into a different person overnight. However, there are specific steps you can take and information that you can equip yourself with that over time, can completely transform the way you feel about your capabilities and ability to make a meaningful contribution to the world. And in turn, you'll be more willing and better equipped to go after more of the opportunities that you desire.

7 STEPS TO BUILDING AUTHENTIC CONFIDENCE

Step 1: Own Your Expertise

We each have certain talents and abilities that we operate in at a high level. The problem is that many people undervalue what they bring to the table. Some have "showy talents," like extreme intelligence, musical or athletic abilities. But did you know that gifts that you see as ordinary have the potential to change the life or business of someone who lacks them? Just because it comes easy to you doesn't mean it isn't valuable.

Step 2: Embrace the Mission

Get a mental picture in your head of a child that you love. It could be your son or daughter, grandchild, niece or nephew, or the child of a friend. Can you see them?

Now I want you to imagine that child falling overboard into the water with you as their only hope for survival. You're a decent swimmer, but you're not a lifeguard by training. As you stand on the edge of the boat watching this little person you love flailing about, you know that if you don't take action, this person will certainly drown.

Do you jump in? *Of course you do.* You don't spend hours contemplating your skillset. You say to yourself, "I'm good enough, and this child needs me." When the mission is that critical, you don't waste time doubting yourself. You just do it.

What would happen if you lived your life that way? If your commitment to the mission was so strong, you didn't waste time second-guessing yourself?

Think of an opportunity that you shied away from because you didn't feel like you had the right skillset. What was it really about? Was it that you truly lacked the capability needed, or was it the fear of failure?

Often, the fear of failure can be rooted in our own ego. You don't want to look less than perfect. You don't want to be judged. But when you focus on the mission, you take the mental spotlight off yourself and you place it on the people you're serving.

Step 3: Ask for Help

On the other hand, if you were thrown into the deep end of a pool and didn't know how to swim, how realistic would it be to expect yourself to gracefully breaststroke to the other end? Yet, when you're thrown in the deep in professionally — asked to do something for which you're completely unprepared — you expect yourself to execute flawlessly on your own.

Not feeling equipped to deliver on what's being asked of you can take a toll on your self-confidence. Asking for help may feel like a sign of weakness, and depending on the politics of the situation, you may need to think through how to get the help you need while managing your personal brand.

Here are a few strategies to get the help you need:

Ask for Clarification

When framed as the need for clarification, your questions don't have to come across that you're clueless, but that you simply want to make sure you're on the same page. This could sound like, "Who are the stakeholders that will be affected by this?" That information can give you specific people to seek out to get their take on what needs to happen. Or "If this assignment is executed successfully, what would the outcomes look like?" Then, you can begin with the end in mind and work backwards.

Focus on Professional Development

I'm not a fan of "fake it till you make it." Instead, how about investing in yourself so you can deliver results that you can confidently stand on? No matter how little time or resources you're working with, you have tools within your reach for continuous improvement.

Here are a few suggestions:

- Find a mentor in your line of work whom you feel safe with taking your "stupid questions" to without fear of judgement. They may be in another department or outside of your organization altogether. Think of former colleagues, educators, or members of organizations you belong to.
- Attend conferences or workshops sponsored by professional organizations even if your company won't pay for it. Invest in yourself.
- Subscribe to podcasts and listen to audiobooks as an efficient and inexpensive way to expand your knowledge and stay on top of what's happening in your industry. Check with your public library to find out if they offer free audiobook rentals.
- If you're feeling underdeveloped in certain areas, look for ways to gain new experiences in a low-pressure environment, such as volunteering in the community or your church. I have a friend who built such a strong skillset and tangible results in online community engagement by managing the women's ministry online book club at her church that she ended up being hired to do it by a growing company.

A Special Note for Business Owners

If your clients request deliverables from you that are outside of your lane, don't fake it. Be honest and let them know that the request is outside of the scope of the services you perform and refer them to someone else, or partner with someone who has that skillset. That way, you keep your customers happy and support another entrepreneur. Saying yes and fumbling your way through the work will make you question your value because you don't know if you're doing it right, causing your confidence to take a hit. However, if you have a strong desire to build that skillset and your client is willing to take the risk of allowing you to figure it out, go for it.

Here's the bottom line: You don't know everything. And you won't always be able to run from situations that put you outside of your comfort zone. But you don't have to figure it out all by yourself, either. Find safe ways to ask for help and celebrate yourself for developing new skills.

Step 4: Take Risks

When I decided to move to Texas as a single mom with a 5-year-old, there were plenty of people who tried to talk me out of it. Just like there were folks who thought I was crazy to start a business in the middle of a recession. When I was finishing my first book in 2012, one of my best friends was afraid that it wouldn't turn out well within the short timeframe I gave myself to complete it and that my reputation would suffer.

None of these situations turned out perfectly. I remember lying on my couch in a puddle of tears on Christmas Day because my son was back in Michigan with his dad while I was on-call for work in Texas. I've also had plenty of financial ups and downs since launching my business 2009. And my first book? I ended up changing the cover design after it was originally published.

Still, I don't regret any of the risks I took. I'd make the same decisions today if it was between that and playing it safe. We all have different levels of risk tolerance. Some people will pack up their cars and move cross-country or quit their jobs on a whim. Others may spend years researching and contemplating but never make a decision to pursue what they really want. The best place is probably somewhere in the middle.

We often fear risks because we desire predictability. We want to know if we do X, then Y will happen. But that's not the way life works. By routinely taking risks, we can lessen our need for certainty. If you're an entrepreneur or plan to be one in the future, know this: Uncertainty is certain. However, every risk doesn't have to be life-altering. It's about making it normal to do things that scare you.

For example, I'm afraid of heights. To even stand on the second floor of a shopping mall and look below makes me nauseous. By the time I was a teenager, I realized that my fear was going to cause me to miss out on a lot of things that I wanted to do. Growing up in Michigan, it was always a treat to cross over into Ohio to visit an amusement park called Cedar Point. Even though I'm afraid of heights, I'm also an adrenaline junkie, so I had to ride the biggest roller coaster in the park. I'd have butterflies in my stomach with every turn of the massive line as I contemplated walking away. But I always stayed in line, rode the ride, and had the time of my life.

What is fear causing you to miss out on? Are you missing opportunities to share your knowledge or wisdom on bigger platforms, like Maggie? Playing small in your business, like Alicia? Staying in the safety of a less-than-fulfilling career, like Michael?

I challenge you to answer the following questions:
1. What would you do if fear wasn't a factor?
2. What are you afraid of? (keep asking yourself this question until you uncover all of your fears)
3. What would happen if each of these fears were realized?
4. What could happen if you were successful? (keep asking yourself this question until you run out of answers)
5. What would happen if all of your successes were realized?

The reality is this: Everything you attempt won't turn out the way you want it to. You might not get the promotion you apply for. You could host an event and five people show up. Someone else may win the contract that your business is after. When we don't get what we want, a safe response is to say, "Well, I guess this just isn't in the cards for me." But that isn't necessarily true. Sometimes we're just not the best candidate. Maybe your marketing plan sucks. But that doesn't mean *you* suck. Figure out what you need to do to get closer to the results you desire and actually do it.

Routinely taking risks can help you to overcome the fear of failure and rejection. Sometimes the greatest risk is not taking one.

Step 5: Get Comfortable in Your Own Skin

I'm one of five co-hosts on a podcast called Clear Talk. Every quarter, we have a professional photo shoot to capture images to use in promotions for the show. If you've ever seen me, you know I'm not built like a supermodel. And after I crossed the 40 mark, picking up weight became a whole lot easier and getting it off has gotten a whole lot harder. I make eating healthy and getting physical activity a priority, but my weight is not something I obsess over...until this particular photo shoot.

ONPURPOSE / **12** Strategies to Reclaim Your Power and Change Your Life

When our producer sent the picture that he planned to use in an upcoming promo, I almost cried. I looked terrible and the whole world was going to see me looking terrible, where it would be retrievable on social media forever and ever. I couldn't ask him not to use the photo because the other ladies looked great. I wanted to quit.

It sounds crazy, right? Quit a show because I took a bad picture? Sure, that wouldn't be the given reason. But if we don't uproot those insecurities, we start looking for excusable reasons for our decision. All of a sudden, you're too busy. Or as Michael in the beginning of the chapter put it, with so much uncertainly in the economy, the safest move was to stay in his current role.

What is Michael's real reason for turning his back on his dream job? He's gained nearly 100 pounds over the past five years and is very insecure about his personal appearance. As much as he loves being out in the community and would jump at any opportunity to speak to an audience, it only exacerbates the anguish he already feels about just getting dressed for work in the morning.

I've never met anyone who is 100% happy with everything about their physical appearance. That's why the health and beauty industries rake in billions of dollars each year. The question is, what can you do to feel more confident with your personal appearance?

This isn't about vanity. When you feel like you look good, you exude confidence. Why are people always beaming on makeover shows? Whether consciously or unconsciously, you might be talking yourself out of opportunities more often than you realize because you're afraid of being judged regarding your appearance:

- I look too old, and they'll write me off as a has-been.
- I look too young, and they'll think I don't know anything.
- I'm too fat.

- I'm too short.
- Taking care of my body is a priority, and they'll assume I'm not smart or committed to my job.
- I don't have expensive clothes and won't look like I "belong."
- They'll judge me as elitist or out of touch because I like nice things.

As you can see, it's impossible to make everyone happy. You can't control how others feel about you. But you can control how you feel about yourself. If there are things that you are insecure about related to your personal appearance and you have the power to change them so you can feel better about yourself, then give yourself that gift. It could be something as simple as getting up thirty minutes earlier to be intentional about putting yourself together for the day or picking your clothes out before you go to bed.

If you don't know what your best look is, I HIGHLY recommend hiring a stylist. You can find one that fits your budget! Knowing how to dress for your body type and being able to easily go to a few looks in your closet that you feel good in could be the difference in you showing up or bowing out.

Step 6: Change Your Internal Narrative

No matter how good you are at what you do or how great you look, you will never believe it if you're telling yourself that it isn't true.

When was the last time you paid close attention to your internal dialogue? Would you say the things that you say to yourself are the same things you would say to someone you care about? Capture those thoughts that are out of alignment with who you are or who you want to be. You may find writing specific affirmations for yourself to be effective at reframing your inner voice.

Along the same lines, do your best not to internalize constructive feedback. If someone points out that there is an area where you can improve, it doesn't mean you're a failure, it's simply a data point. Reflect on that data point and consider if it is something to work on in your personal development journey.

Step 7: Focus on Progress, Not Perfection

At the time of this writing, I'm two months in from purchasing a Peloton stationary exercise bike. One of the things I love about Peloton is that there are several ways to track your progress. When you're on the bike, you can look at the leaderboard to see your real-time progress against everyone who has ever taken that ride, or you can compete against yourself. When I looked at the all-time leaderboard, I often completed the ride discouraged because of my low ranking compared to everyone else. But once I started filtering it against my previous rides, it became all about simply doing better than I did the last time.

How do you set expectations for yourself? Are you looking at the veterans in your company or industry, kicking yourself because you don't feel as smart or accomplished as them when they may have decades worth of experience on you?

What could be different for you if you only measure yourself against yourself? Sure, look to people who have set an example that you'd like to follow, but if you're scoring yourself against someone else, you might not realize they're playing an entirely different game. Do you know how much they have invested in being where they are today? Do you know what sacrifices they've made? Could they have had factors working in their favor that don't exist for you? You don't know the whole story, so just focus on yourself. Set challenging, but realistic milestones for yourself based on where you are, where you want to go, and what you're willing to do to get there.

CONCLUSION: LIVING YOUR CONFIDENT LIFE

Even when you're confident, you believe in yourself, and you ask for what you want, things won't always pan out. But you can't let that change the way you see yourself. You can't let it keep you from wanting and pursuing more. The answer won't always be yes, but if you're not confident enough to ask, it will ALWAYS be no. Know when it's time to get out of your head and take action. Trust yourself. Invest in yourself. Keep getting better. That's how authentic confidence is built.

Want more tips on building a personal brand rooted in authentic confidence so you don't shy away when your next big opportunity comes? Download my free resource at **MyBrandOnPurpose.com.**

PUT IT INTO PRACTICE
7 Affirmations for Fighting Fear

1. I will embrace, appreciate and respect my expertise by owning my natural abilities. I am positioned to share my unique story and gifts with others because I have something valuable to bring to the table.
2. I refuse to waste precious time doubting myself when others desperately need my skill set. I believe the mission is more important than my ego.
3. I don't have to figure out everything alone. I can tap into the strength of my inner circle and trusted experts by asking for help and celebrating each opportunity to learn new skills.
4. I will normalize attempting new things that take me out of my comfort zone because I know the growth I'll experience is worth the discomfort that comes when I confront the fear that holds me back.
5. I will not allow my insecurities to excuse me from fulfilling my mission. I accept that I can't control how others feel about me, but I will lovingly commit to caring for myself without pressuring myself to meet impossible standards.
6. I will not internalize poorly delivered feedback or cut myself down with negative self-talk. Instead, I will reframe my inner voice by affirming the good placed in me and by speaking those thoughts that align with who I aim to become.
7. I will celebrate my progress and continue toward growth by setting challenging, but realistic milestones for myself based on where I am, where I want to go, and what I'm willing to do to realize my goals.

Download exercise from the "Resources for Readers" section, password "Reader" at PlatformforPurposeBook.com.

ONPURPOSE / 12 Strategies to Reclaim Your Power and Change Your Life

Learn About
VERONICA ARMSTRONG

Whether she's coaching leadership teams, executives, or women who simply desire to break out of their invisible box so they can live life on their terms, Veronica's mission is to help women find the clarity and confidence they need to go after the opportunities they deserve.

Veronica is the founder of Leadership Life Support, which she created to help professional women become better leaders from the inside out. She's now extended her services to support women taking responsibility for their lives so they can live life on their terms.

A certified life and leadership coach, entrepreneur, and corporate executive, Veronica brings value from both her professional and personal experiences, including a life of verbal and physical abuse and three years as a ward of the state being shuffled from group homes to foster homes, before making it to the e-suite in corporate America.

An Ossining, NY, native, Veronica now resides in the Phoenix area, where she enjoys roller skating, reading, and hanging out with her husband and son. You can connect with Veronica on your favorite social media networks and subscribe to her blog at leadershiplifesupport.com.

Connect with Veronica Armstrong

Website: LeadershipLifeSupport.com
Email: Veronica@LeadershipLifeSupport.com

Chapter Four
Seven Ingredients to a Secret Sauce:
Leave Behind Limiting Beliefs to Embrace a Mindset of Success

by Veronica Armstrong

I was ripped from my home at the age of twelve and became a ward of the state for the next three years. During that time, I was shuffled to and from group homes, foster care, and a detention center. Coming from a small town of twenty-five thousand people, I was not prepared to learn and experience some of what I was exposed to. Being confined in institutions with teens accused of arson, assault and battery, and a host of other crimes was frightening, especially for a twelve-year-old whose only crimes were not consistently following her mother's rules and breaking into her home after her mother locked her out.

I spent most of my childhood trying to understand why the world seemed so cruel and dreaming about how to free myself from what felt like perpetual misery. I felt unloved, disliked, and discarded by the adults charged with my care. They were supposed to protect me and be good examples to emulate. Instead, they exposed me to limiting beliefs and negative experiences that began to shape the way I viewed myself and my future.

Although your circumstances may have been different, maybe you can relate to my story. Maybe you were born to a mother who left you to fend for yourself or move in with relatives. If you were born to parents who never achieved much beyond high school, you may lack the knowledge to help you overcome a similar fate. Maybe you were born into a situation where you were the primary caregiver to younger siblings, and as a result, you had to put all of your childhood dreams on the shelf.

Have years in a dysfunctional environment and negative experiences left you with limiting beliefs about yourself and your future?

Luckily for me, I had a turning point that propelled me into the future I longed for. This was one of the first steps to put me on a path that would help me overcome my dysfunctional past.

I became an emancipated minor by the time I was fifteen due to the loving care and concern of a 25-year-old law student intern named Mary. Mary saw something in me. She believed in me. She felt strongly that I was not where I was supposed to be. She told me there was more for me in the world and I should believe that I could do and be anything that I wanted. Mary's words of encouragement and her act of kindness would stick with me for the rest of my life. After high school, I went directly to college where I began to follow a path to a better future. My friends in college, who had much more stable backgrounds than mine, influenced how I perceived what was achievable. I became increasingly hopeful that the changes I longed for had a chance of coming to fruition.

One step at a time, I began to leave behind the limiting beliefs that held me back to embrace a new mindset that set me on a path to success. Eventually, I reached milestones that I never would have imagined — I earned a bachelor's degree, then a master's degree, and eventually become a corporate executive!

Transformation Starts with a Choice

Sometimes, when I look back at my childhood and remember some of the hard places, I'm amazed at my transformation. The journey of being a directionless teen to becoming a respected corporate executive has been amazing. I've shared some of my story with you so you, too can believe in a better future and experience success for yourself.

The reality is that many of us have negative experiences that shape our behavior and limit how we view the world. We each have a choice: We can let the past limit us or we can choose transformation.

I love this quote from Oprah Winfrey that confirms that the choice to change starts within: *"It doesn't matter who you are, where you came from. The ability to triumph begins with you. Always."*

I made a choice to believe I would no longer be defined by limiting beliefs to believing I have what it takes to be successful. I call this mindshift my *Secret Sauce*.

I believe this mindshift will work for you, just like it worked for me, by transforming you from defeated by your past to hopeful that you can accomplish the success you desire. Before we look at the ingredients in the secret sauce, let me warn you — transformation takes work. And doing the work can be difficult because we'll need to face our demons and fears, acknowledge our faults, and learn things about ourselves that we didn't know.

We'll need to change some of our ways, alter how we see the world, and let go of limiting beliefs. But I promise you, by doing the hard work, you can leave behind limiting beliefs and move forward to an amazing and fulfilling life. Now let's take a look at the Secret Sauce.

THE SEVEN INGREDIENTS IN THE SECRET SAUCE

#1: Take the Reins and Responsibility for Your Life

No matter what we want to be in life or what we want to do, it's important that we find the courage to take the reins and become the leader of our lives. We can't blame our parents, childhood experiences, or traumatic events for our current position in life because our current position is only temporary. I've found that forgiving people in the past and forgiving ourselves are important ingredients in the secret sauce.

Change comes to those who are fearless and who take control. We must do the work to reverse the effects of traumatic childhood experiences. Change comes to those who lay the foundation on which to build a secure future. Without doing the work, we could be squandering our God-given talents.

#2: Get to Know the Person in the Mirror

It's easy to look in the mirror every morning without the slightest idea of who the person is looking back at us. We see her every flaw, we know what she is thinking, and we know how she feels. We do not talk to her; we look at her in judgment. We have lived with her every day of our lives, but oddly, we don't know her well. We never ask her who she is.

I can tell you who she is: She's the perfectly imperfect teen who made it to adulthood. She has big goals and dreams. She wants to do something and be someone. She wants to feel like she has a purpose in this world, and she wants to make a difference. We must get to know that girl in the mirror because she can be our guide on this journey to fulfillment.

She is you; you are responsible for her. The person looking back at you in the mirror is dependent upon you to make decisions that will lead her in the direction she wants. If you don't take care of the person looking back at you in the mirror, who will?

Self-awareness is the first step in getting to know ourselves so we can take control of our lives. Knowing ourselves contributes to our successes and our failures. More importantly, self-awareness provides a clear understanding of what we need most to develop in ourselves, our family, and our work teams. We'll gain insights to help us identify skill gaps that might hinder our success and aid us in uncovering our strengths.

> **Surrounding ourselves with people who are already where we want to be will serve as a constant motivator to keep moving forward.**

If you would like a step-by-step guide to help you develop self-awareness, I have a free resource for you. All you need to do is to go to **http://bit.ly/LLS-self-awareness-guide** to download the guide and get started.

#3: Determine Your Passions
When we uncover our passions, we'll find what motivates and drives us. Building our lives around what we're passionate about leads to a life that is fulfilling beyond measure. Working in a field that we are passionate about will help us have the energy, stamina, and drive that will make us a star. When we are passionate about everything we do, life is easier.

#4: Create a Plan to Follow Your Dreams
Once we determine who we are, what we're passionate about, and what our strengths and weaknesses are, it's time to create a development plan. Development plans are not just for the corporate environment. Development plans are useful for anyone on a mission. With a plan, we can set

small goals, track accomplishments, and measure progress daily, weekly, monthly, and quarterly. Whatever you do, I think it's a good idea to write down your larger goals, break them down into smaller action steps, create a plan, and follow it until you achieve your goals.

#5: Find a Mentor or Coach
My personal and professional success has been largely due to having mentors and coaches to help me during my personal development journey. Mentors have given me insight, advice, and support that guided me to make the right decisions. Whether it was a promotion or move out of state, my mentors have helped me see what I sometimes could not see when I needed to make critical decisions that impacted my life.

I've also had an executive coach who helped me during my time as a VP at a large corporation, and I have a life coach who helps me be a better life coach. Let's not forget a business coach who helps me with developing my business. It's beneficial to have a mentor or coach as a neutral party in our corner for the sole purpose of assisting us in staying focused on moving toward our goals.

#6: Surround Yourself with People Who Are Where You Want to Be
Surrounding ourselves with people who are already where we want to be will serve as a constant motivator to keep moving forward. More importantly, this provides an opportunity to accelerate learning and growth as we learn from people who are already doing what we want to do.

#7: Get Out of the Way and Watch Life Unfold
When we finally decide to take control and go after our dreams, then we need to let go, let God, and believe in ourselves. We've made a choice; now we need to follow the plan. We can't allow self-doubt to seep into our minds, and we cannot allow others to deter us from creating an amazing life.

Leave Behind Limiting Beliefs to Embrace a Mindset of Success

As Kobe Bryant once said, "*When you make a choice and say, 'Come hell or high water, I am going to be this,' then you should not be surprised when you are that. It should not be something that is intoxicating or out of character because you have seen this moment for so long that ... when that moment comes, of course it is here because it has been here the whole time, because it has been [in your mind] the whole time.*"

In my career, I have met far too many women who have big dreams, yet they do little to move forward. They want to become leaders, but they don't know where to start. They are too afraid to dream big, too scared to ask for what they want, and they're confused about what to do or where to turn. They don't want to settle for a mediocre life, but they're not sure how to move forward.

Many women ask me how I managed to get to where I am. They ask me what they should do so they can achieve higher levels of success. They want to know my secret. I share the ingredients of the Secret Sauce with my clients and now I'm sharing them with you. When you choose to leave behind a limiting mindset and do the hard work of transformation, you'll find the success you've longed for and imagined.

If you're ready for someone to come alongside you as you start living the life you were born to live, become the executive you've always wanted to be, or become a better leader, let's have a conversation so we can map out a plan that will help you determine a way forward. Go to my website at **leadershiplifesupport.com** and schedule a discovery call. You won't regret your decision!

ON PURPOSE / **12** Strategies to Reclaim Your Power and Change Your Life

PUT IT INTO PRACTICE
The Secret Sauce Manifesto

I believe that transformation starts with a choice.

Today, I choose to believe that I have what it takes to be successful.

I'm prepared to face my demons and fears, acknowledge my faults, and do the hard work to see my vision realized.

Today, I take the reins and responsibility for my life by moving forward with forgiveness and fearlessness.

As I grow in self-awareness, I will nurture myself through better decision-making and the support of my trusted family and mentors.

I surround myself with motivators and learn from my setbacks so that I can continue to press on into the life I was created to live.

Download exercise from the "Resources for Readers" section, password "Reader" at PlatformforPurposeBook.com.

Leave Behind Limiting Beliefs to Embrace a Mindset of Success

Learn About
Clifford Starks

Clifford Starks is a retired professional mixed martial arts fighter who competed for eight years before stepping away from the ring to start a family with his wife.

Clifford believes the journey of transformation includes mind, body and business. All three play key roles in success, as he has learned through his journey as a fighter, competitor, and coach. Today, as a personal trainer, life coach and author of the book, Awaken the Superhero in You, he helps clients focus on their mind, body, and spirit to live happier, more fulfilled lives. Clifford has always been fascinated with psychology which he studies in detail, while also pulling from personal life experiences.

A graduate of Arizona State University, Clifford ranked third in the PAC 10 Conference as a wrestler while earning a degree in kinesiology. Always challenging himself to improve, he continues to compete in Brazilian Jiu Jitsu

Connect with Clifford Starks
Website: CliffordStarks.com
Email: cliff@mindbodymentoring.com

Chapter Five

How to Bounce Back from Setbacks

by Clifford Starks

Did you know that your brain and children's playdough share something in common? Just as playdough is impressed and shaped by tiny fingers, your brain is shaped and molded by your experiences. This malleability enables your brain to learn, grow, and adapt. By the same token, the brain can remain stuck in unhealthy patterns, shaped by negative habits, and, if left unchanged, its adaptation can cast us in a state of misery. Because of the brain's adaptability, we may not even know that it's happening.

Can you see the significant influence our personal experiences and habits have over how we think and who we become? My guess is that, like me, you've had your share of both positive and negative life experiences. Like a potter's gentle touch, life's highs can beautifully shape and nurture our minds. In contrast, our disappointments and wounds can deform and distort them.

Have you ever felt stuck in your life or like there was a barrier you couldn't quite get past? Maybe it was a new job position you were unfamiliar with, or felt was outside of your capability? Or perhaps you've experienced a traumatic event and you simply can't see a way to recover from it.

While these devastating experiences can feel defining and inescapable, their control over us can be broken if we take advantage of our brain's malleability!

Over the next few pages, I'll show how to use that to your advantage so you can overcome your own setbacks. I'll share an embarrassing, but life-changing experience of my own and teach you the 5-Step Bounce Back Blueprint that helped me recover from it.

THE 5-STEP BOUNCE BACK BLUEPRINT

Many people have described "disappointment" as a cruel blow dealt by life. In my case, it's more than a metaphor. As a rookie boxer in the best shape of my life, I was literally knocked out...on LIVE television!

I did everything within my power to prepare for the fight, yet the outcome was completely unlike what I had envisioned. Similarly in life, you may think things are going well until something hits you unexpectedly and turns your world upside down. By taking time to absorb my 5-Step Bounce Back Blueprint, you'll discover how to return to your empowered state in moments when the odds feel stacked against you.

Step 1: Ask yourself, "Where's my hang-up?"

With a captive audience both live and virtually, I believed that being knocked out was a total problem for me. No boxer wants to be knocked down —let alone knocked out especially in front of a large audience of people. My hang-up was that being knocked out felt like a hopelessly embarrassing situation, and I was convinced that no good could come of it. Can you relate?

When you feel stuck or unable to move past a life event, it's important to ask yourself, "What's my hang-up?" Understanding your hang-up is a game changer, because with understanding our problem comes the freedom to proactively adjust, taking you to a better place in your life.

Step 2: Build a Case

There were many reasons getting knocked was a legitimate problem for me. First, my winning record became tarnished by the knockout loss. Of course, this also meant I would only receive half of the prize money for losing. In the weeks that followed, countless friends expressed their pity and sympathy towards me. And my poor wife? She was scared out of her mind!

I desperately wanted to hit the reset button on everything that happened. I trained so hard, but it didn't go the way I planned. After putting my blood, sweat, and tears into winning, I came away from that knockout feeling utterly defeated. And those feelings felt warranted and justified.

Let's shift back to you.

May I walk you through a quick exercise to help you gain clarity on why your hang-up is holding you back? Let's pretend we're going to put your "hang-up" on trial. I want you to become the prosecutor and defender of this pervasive thought. Start with asking yourself the following:

- Does your hang-up feel like a problem?
- Is it possible that others are making you feel like it's a problem?
- If you do feel it is a problem, why do you feel that way?
- What would a solution look like?

Do your best to answer these questions as deeply as possible. Your honest responses will help you uncover the truth about your situation. This is the key to seeing a breakthrough, because you cannot find a solution to your problem without first understanding it.

Step 3: Confirm Whether Your Belief is True or False

Following the knockout, I was left with a decision to make: Yes, I lost the match, but would I allow my defeat to define who I was moving forward? I knew that perceiving my experience as a loss would do nothing for me. Putting so much into something and walking away as the loser, I knew this perception would only be real if I chose to make it so. Being a winner or a loser all starts with one's head space.

If you feel like a loser it will show in your tone, speech, and body language. The same is true with feeling like a winner. Although I lost the match, I was not a loser. That's why I held my head high and decided to embrace a winner's mindset. I was going to bounce back from this setback just as I did in the past. This confident and hopeful thinking instantly made me stand taller and prouder.

When we build a case for our hang-up, we're really determining whether it is true or if it's poor self-talk that we've made out to be true. In my case, it was true that I lost the match, but that didn't mean that I was, by nature, a loser. You can come to some very deep realizations on this step and opening up the mind to possibilities is big here, so I congratulate you on going through the process.

Step 4: Become Solution-Focused

I knew I had to change my perspective about my experience, so I began shifting my focus from the problem to my solution moving forward. "Okay. That embarrassing knock-out happened, but what solutions do I have? How can this loss become a gain in my favor?" I asked myself.

First, I discovered that by embracing my experience, I could use my story as a powerful testimony to motivate others. We often wonder how we'd handle getting knocked-down in a metaphorical sense, but my real experience of being knocked-out afforded me the opportunity to see how I would handle the challenge put right in front of me. With that perspective, I was excited about the prospect of standing up stronger than I was before and learning from the recovery process.

> **Being a winner or a loser all starts with one's head space.**

When I shifted my focus from my hang-up to my solution moving forward, my experience was no longer a loss — it was a lesson. A lesson that said, "Hey Clifford Starks, what are you going to do when you get knocked out? Are you just going to quit?" My reply was, "No, I'm not going to quit! I am going to come back stronger than before!"

When you experience a hang-up, I invite you to think deeply about your stumbling blocks and look for potential solutions — openings and paths you can take to press forward. Ask yourself, "Is there something I need to learn?" Maybe there's someone who overcame a similar struggle that can help you over the hurdle. What actions have you taken to help you with the problem? The more open you are to finding a solution, the sooner those solutions will come. Believe in yourself, because I believe in you. There is definitely a solution to your problem.

Step 5: Put in the Work

Since the brain doesn't exactly like being knocked out, Step Five was rather difficult for me. I wasted no time getting back into my boxer's conditioning routine, but sparring against a partner was a real challenge for me. During those grueling moments, I remembered that my story was not just for me. It was for anyone who has ever been knocked out in life or anything for that matter! Every time I trained I thought about the promise I made to myself and to everyone else. I put in the work. I trained to sharpen my craft. I improved my skill set and stretched myself so I could come back stronger than ever.

Once you find your solution, it's time to execute or put your solution into practice. It's said that "Practice makes perfect," so practice to the best of your ability. Do your best to be your best. Half-effort practice leads to terrible results, so if you're going to practice at it, make it count.

Finally, remember that the best execution happens when you choose to focus on one step of your solution at a time. Enlist an accountability partner or mentor as an extra set of eyes watch you throughout your process. We do our best, but often we don't know what we don't know. So let your accountability partner know what you want to work on and have them check in with you regularly to see if you've followed through.

RECOVERY & RESILIENCE

While it felt like a huge loss in the moment, bouncing back from my knock-out experience transformed me into a capable fighter. After returning to the ring, I ended up winning five fights straight after that and even got the opportunity to compete for the World Series of Fighting title.

Bouncing back taught me that a loss doesn't define who I am. I get to choose how I show up after defeat. When I view a loss as a learning experience instead of a defeat, I have the opportunity to grow stronger. Because I shifted my mind off of my hang-up and on to my solution, I was able to win five fights in a row afterward. My knock-out wasn't the first road block I've experienced and it certainly won't be my last, but this 5-step process has helped me recover time and time again.

Your possibilities are limitless. After a hang-up, I want to see you get back into your ring just as I did. Define your hang-up, examine it, determine if it's true or false, focus on your solution, and work for the results you desire. While it may not be "Boxing Champion," there's a title waiting for you somewhere.

I hope this strategy serves you well on your journey. If this resonates with you, I would like to invite you a step closer to continue to gain insights and achieve the results you are looking for in your life.

Email me at **cliff@mindbodymentoring.com** and tell me where you would like to be next year along with your greatest challenge and I will provide you with insight to help guide you in the right direction.

Remember, greatness starts with a thought and then an action on that thought. Will you take action?

ONPURPOSE / **12** Strategies to Reclaim Your Power and Change Your Life

PUT IT INTO PRACTICE
Bounce-Back Journal Prompts

What's your hang-up?

_____

_____

_____

Why is this a problem for you?

_____

_____

_____

Is it possible that others are making you feel like it's a problem? If so, how?

_____

_____

_____

If you do feel it is a problem, why do you feel that way?

_____

_____

_____

In one sentence, what toxic statement is this problem speaking over you?

_____

_____

_____

Is this statement a truth worth living out? Or is it a false narrative that you've given influence over your life?

_____
_____
_____

What actions have you taken to resolve this problem?

_____
_____
_____

How can you practically choose to GROW through what you're presently GOing through?

_____
_____
_____

Moving forward, what actions will you take to bounce back from this? Who will hold you accountable?

_____
_____
_____

Download exercise from the "Resources for Readers" section, password "Reader" at PlatformforPurposeBook.com.

ON PURPOSE / 12 Strategies to Reclaim Your Power and Change Your Life

Learn About
La'Vista Jones

La'Vista Jones is a multifaceted resource, helping her clients bring order to the chaos of life and business. She believes her clients can learn how the price of success doesn't have to include burnout or broken promises to themselves. By discovering a better way to run a business, clients learn to make themselves and what they love a priority.

As an author, speaker, strategist, and coach, La'Vista is leading a movement of women who want more from life than frazzled days and sleepless nights. La'Vista has an inspiring message that challenges the archaic and often coveted idea of work-life balance. Her unique magic is helping women get 'ish done, without burning themselves out.

La'Vista is the founder and CEO of 31 Marketplace, an agency that blends systemization and self-care, making both simple, personal, and effective.

Although she is a proud native of Ohio, La'Vista currently resides in Arizona. She enjoys living life with her favorite guys — her college sweetheart and husband Stewart; their son, publicly known as The Cub; and their Mastiff fur baby, Bulldozer.

Connect with La'Vista Jones
Website: LavistaJones.com
Email: support@thirtyonemarketplace.com

Chapter Six

Reconnect with Your Joy Through Self-Care

by La'Vista Jones

A few years ago, I attended a women's conference at my church. All the participants sat around tables that included eight to ten other women. Throughout the conference, we participated in structured table talks led by the designated facilitator at each table. During one of those talks, the facilitator at my table led us through a discussion topic around needing to have a better theology of fun — code for self-care.

While the women at my table unanimously agreed that engaging in fun was essential to their overall self-care, they each had trouble identifying the unique things that they personally enjoyed doing for fun.

When the initial question about what we each like to do for fun was first asked, there was an awkward silence, and each of the women at the table looked around at each other before anyone provided an answer. Here are a few of the responses as the dialogue resumed:

- "My husband likes to go to the movies, so we go together."
- "I spend a lot of time with my kids traveling for their soccer league."
- "To be honest, I really don't know."

Not one response was dedicated to something that brought one of those women joy as a unique, individual person — they all had something to do with someone else.

Did this surprise me? Nope. But it did make my heart ache, because the responses illustrated how the natural progression of increased relational equity with others is often paired with a decreased personal connection with self. In my experience working with women and in living my own life, I've observed that it can be very easy to forget to make time for the little things that make you - you.

Now I'm sure that each of the ladies sitting at that table with me during that conference found enjoyment in doing the fun things that they talked about alongside their spouses and children. But when you think of writing out your own joy list and identifying the things that bring you true pleasure and happiness, would sitting for hours on a soccer field make the cut? When you fill your schedule with other people's priorities, it doesn't leave much or any time for you to be your own priority.

My experience at the conference was the catalyst that sent me on a mission to help other women define self-care for themselves and rediscover their joy list.

DEFINING SELF-CARE

So let's get back to the basics of you. This starts with how you define self-care.

As I began to look closer at the self-care examples so readily marketed, I realized that I wasn't seeing anything that actually resonated with me or my current season in life. It became clear that the core definition of self-care is not necessarily what we see on social media or in magazines, because self-care is not a one-size-fits-all experience.

Armed with that revelation, I knew I had to do two things to make self-care successful for myself:

- Define self-care on my own terms
- Identify activities that would support me in living out that definition

Embarking on my own self-care journey, I discovered that while I enjoyed receiving a relaxing massage or taking a luxury bomb-infused bubble bath, I also found that little ordinary things in life sparked joy.

I knew there had to be something more to that. So I kept scheduling time for my massages and baths, but I also began to pay more attention to the little things.

Looking down to see my painted nails as I typed an email to a client put a smile on my face. So I started to hold space on my calendar to shop for nail stickers and embellishments as well as at-home nail art time.

Wearing the perfume that my husband gave me as a birthday gift reminded me that I was treasured as a wife. So I made it a point to put that bottle of perfume on my bathroom counter as a reminder to use it. What was I saving it for anyway? Isn't every day that I'm alive reason enough to celebrate with a spritz of the good stuff?

Sitting down and spending face-to-face time with my son during lunch, uninterrupted by the television or cell phones, and listening to him giggle literally feeds my soul. So I began scheduling lunch on my calendar to protect those special moments.

Taking moments at the beginning of a day to breathe deeply and set my intentions made me feel better and more equipped to tackle the day ahead. So I purposefully added a breathing ritual to my morning routine, the perfect companion to my coffee.

ONPURPOSE / **12** Strategies to Reclaim Your Power and Change Your Life

When I started paying attention to all the ways I found joy in the ordinary, I knew I had discovered it — my own definition of self-care. I define self-care as enjoying those consistent and purposeful moments in life that make me feel good and bring me joy.

Now, I want you to imagine that you're sitting with me at that women's conference, and I want you to take a few moments to write down your own definition of self-care.

I define self-care as:

_____

_____

_____

You did it!

Defining self-care on your own terms is just the beginning. Now it is time to craft your joy list.

CRAFTING YOUR JOY LIST

Depending on how much time you've previously thought about the trendy topic of self-care, creating your personal definition of it may have been a relatively easy question for you to answer.

So let's dive deeper. If you were given a full 48 hours to spend just to focus on your own self-care, what would you do during that time?

Reconnect with Your Joy Through Self-Care

Write down what living out your own self-care care would look like during these 48 hours:

_____
_____
_____
_____
_____
_____

Was that question a little harder to answer?

Probably. And here's why:

Over time, as we get older and develop more significant relationships and build successful careers and businesses, we can gradually lose touch with what I call our joy list. Your joy list is composed of all the things you engage in that truly bring you great pleasure and happiness.

As you develop relationships with others, especially romantic ones, you tend to start taking more of an interest in the things on their joy list to increase the time you can spend with them. As your family expands, you invest time in helping your children realize and cultivate their own joy lists. As you experience professional growth, you make personal sacrifices to support the long game of your ambition.

How does this gradual disconnection from your joy list play out in real life? It looks a lot like skipping out on your regular time sipping coffee at your favorite bookstore on Saturday mornings, because that hottie you're falling for would rather go hiking. Eventually you can't remember the last time you sat and read a book.

It looks a lot like unapologetically spending $300 on your

Little's upcoming soccer season and yet feeling immense internal guilt for merely thinking about buying yourself those jeans you saw on sale for $45 — even though the last pair of jeans you bought are from two years ago and fit you terribly.

It looks a lot like saying yes to late nights in the office, more and more frequently, and missing family dinners — even though one of your core values is anchored in spending quality time with your family.

So, what do you like to do for fun? You should be the undisputed expert on this topic, but if you find that question a little hard to answer, it's okay. Reconnecting with your joy list is a work in progress.

If you need help with your list, do this: Start writing.

Grab a pen, a journal, calm your mind, and go to town listing out the things that light your fire, make you laugh, and make your heart smile — those things that bring you true pleasure and happiness. That's your joy list.

Write without any editing or judgement. Block the thoughts about what others might think if they saw some of the things on your list — this list is all about you. And if you get stuck with this exercise, remember the wise musings of Dr. Seuss, *"Be who you are and say what you feel, because those who mind don't matter and those who matter don't mind."*

Imagine that your financial resources are as unlimited as you are when it comes to the things you write down. There is a strategy and a budget for anything. But don't think that everything you write down has to be over-the-top and expensive — you can often find joy in the simplest of moments that are absolutely free.

Living out your joy list will expand to the time you give it, so don't be preoccupied about how much time you think everything you put on your list is going to take. Your self-care isn't just one more thing to put on the to-do list; it's a lifestyle. And I know someone that can help you infuse the items on your list into your daily routines — one clue, you're reading her chapter right now.

Your joy list doesn't have to be long, expensive, or risque. But it does have to speak to your heart and capture the essence of who you are and how you're wired to be.

Work on your list right now.

JOY ON YOUR OWN TERMS

How did you enjoy working through those exercises? Defining and living out self-care on your own terms is a game changer. You are no longer caught in the comparison trap of thinking that you are somehow not doing self-care the right way. Instead, you are equipped with a foundation to launch out and live your own joy-filled self-care journey.

Remember, the key to feeling successful in self-care is to apply your own definition and exercise your care through the joy list you created.

I'd love to come alongside you during your self-care journey. Go to **lavistajones.com** to schedule a connection call with me today.

In the meantime, take care of yourself.

PUT IT INTO PRACTICE
Create Your Happy Plan

Let's get back to the basics of you by reconnecting with those things that are fun to you — those things that make you happy and recharge your batteries.

Step One | Schedule & Prioritize Happy Time on Your Calendar

If you're anything like me, you use some form of a planner or perhaps an electronic calendar on your phone to organize all of your appointments and activities in one place. Take a look at your calendar and carve out 2 to 4 blocks of time over the next 30 days that you will utilize for Happy Time or "me" time. Be mindful to prioritize this time just like you would any other important activity on your calendar.

Step Two | Identify Your Happy Stuff

Now work on identifying the things that you really enjoy doing. Think back to activities that brought you happiness as a child, as a teenager, or even as a young adult. These memories will serve as the foundation of the activities you should put on your list to enjoy during your scheduled Happy Time. Once you complete your list, assign one activity to each of the time blocks selected on your calendar.

Step Three | Delight in Your Happy Life

Go enjoy some happiness! When your scheduled Happy Time pops up on your calendar, make sure to fully enjoy the time you've carved out of your schedule for YOU by actually doing the activities that you identified. Try to minimize any distractions and be present in those moments.

At the end of the 30 days, set aside time to do some introspection. Consider how those activities made you feel. Recall any obstacles you encountered that held you back from making the most of your Happy Time. Reflecting on your experience will allow you to make needed adjustments as you plan out your next 30 days of on-purpose happiness.

Keep in mind that it may also bring light to your need for additional support as you push forward towards the transformation of making yourself a priority.

Happy Living!

Download exercise from the "Resources for Readers" section, password "Reader" at PlatformforPurposeBook.com.

ON PURPOSE / 12 Strategies to Reclaim Your Power and Change Your Life

Learn About
Rebecca Barranca

Rebecca (Becky) Barranca, MA is a writer, public speaker, community educator, and women's ministry leader. Her goal is to use her blog, **beckybarrancalivingnaturally.com** to provide a go-to resource for women who are pursuing a more natural and healthier lifestyle for themselves and their family at an accessible cost.

After working as an HR professional, non-profit founder, and an insurance broker for many years and keeping a very hectic schedule, Becky knew she needed to make changes to her family's stressful lifestyle. Since her first baby was born fifteen years ago, she has slowly but surely been able to adapt her household into a less toxic, more organic and natural, relaxed and intentional home atmosphere.

Becky has spent countless hours researching health and natural living topics with a discerning eye. While not a medical professional, she is able to share valuable health information and natural living ideas through classes and speaking engagements. The knowledge that Becky shares empowers individuals to make better informed decisions about their health, nutrition, and the products they choose to use in their homes.

Connect with Rebecca Barranca
Website: beckybarrancalivingnaturally.com
Instagram: @beckyb.naturally

Chapter Seven

Ten Ways to Live a More Natural Life Everyday

by Rebecca Barranca

"If I had only known..."

This is a thought we've all wrestled with at one time or another in the course of our lives. In my case, it weighed heavily on my mind at age 49 when my doctor diagnosed me with leukemia. If I had only known that cancer was looming ahead, I would not have waited until my 30s to start living a more natural and toxin-free lifestyle. Still, I questioned whether I could've prevented this outcome at all.

When it comes to our health, there are so many factors beyond our control, but my experience has taught me that learning to live a more natural lifestyle is the key to maintaining good health. Perhaps like me, you are going about your daily life with some concerns about potential health issues in the back of your mind, but you lack the urgency to make the necessary changes to improve your health in the long-term. Imagine my shock when I went into the doctor's office for thyroid issues but left with a cancer diagnosis.

I'm grateful that leukemia is a slow-growing cancer, but since there are no cures or treatment options available, there isn't much I can actively do to resist this genetic disease. To add to my frustration, medical experts cannot tell me what causes this cancer. As you might imagine, receiving this diagnosis has had a huge impact on my life and certainly on my family and close friends as well. Despite it all, this diagnosis has propelled me into *battle mode* to fight against it, because I want to *live* and prevent others from contracting this disease. For me, that began with abandoning the quick fixes and convenient products I grew accustomed to using in the past, and now I'll invite you to do the same.

Striving to live naturally should be a priority for all of us, and preferably implemented *before* we have a health crisis. While there are so many things you can do to live a more natural life, I will outline my top ten tips here. But my first piece of advice would be to start by giving yourself permission to slow down, relax, and lead a more toxin-free life. Know that it may take weeks, months, or even a couple of years to get to where you want to be, and that's okay! Stay focused, steady, and consistent with these ideas and you will see results.

Step One: Give Up Toxic Cleaning Products

I think it is critical to stop using bleach and other conventional cleaning products in the home. Many of us grew up using bleach to keep things sanitized, but did you know there are natural ingredients that are excellent disinfectants? Bleach is one of the most harmful substances we can use in our home. Not to mention, it can be deadly if mixed with ammonia, hydrogen peroxide, alcohol, or other acidic products.

A report of a study published in The Guardian stated that regular use of bleach and other common disinfectants has been linked to a higher risk of developing fatal lung disease. The 30-year study by Harvard University and the French National Institute of Health and Medical Research found that individuals using the products one time a week had up to a 32% increased chance of developing the condition.[1]

Did you know that currently, the United States law does not require cleaning product companies to fully disclose their ingredients? So, while they say that their products are "natural" there is really no telling what is being used. Yes, you could buy fancy natural disinfectant products (check them carefully because they are not always completely natural), but why not save some cash and try making a do-it-yourself bathroom cleaner?

>Here's a recipe:

>Mix lemon peels with white vinegar in a 2-quart jar, let it sit covered in a dark place for about 2 weeks, then strain out the vinegar into a glass spray bottle and use on bathtubs and toilets. You can use it in conjunction with baking soda for extra scrubbing power. (Just don't use lemon on granite countertops.)

>Or, let the science of chemistry work for you. Using white vinegar and hydrogen peroxide sprayed consecutively (not mixed together) after surfaces have been properly cleaned has been shown to break down germs to the point of halting their proliferation of infection.[2]

Essential oils can also be used for cleaning and disinfecting in your home. I can't say enough about how well they work for so many things.

Next, change your laundry process. Use hydrogen peroxide and baking soda instead of bleach for whites. Do not use fabric softeners, especially not dryer sheets that emit toxins into the air in your home and backyard (as well as your neighbor's). A good alternative to fabric softeners is wool dryer balls, which are non-toxic and are more cost-effective long-term.

Step Two: Cut Out the Sugar

One of the biggest yet unnoticed toxins in our life is sweet and dear to us — sugar. Refined sugar and artificial sweetener products are some of the most harmful ingredients to our bodies! Not only do they promote weight gain and high blood sugar,[3] but they can also damage the collagen in our skin that keeps us looking younger and have been proven to feed cancer cells. Sugar drastically depletes our immune system, so especially in the pandemic crisis, we need to do everything we can to maintain a strong immune system.

I think one of the most common uses of sugar comes from drinking sodas, sugar-laden coffees, and coffee house latte teas. Try changing your beverages over to homemade infused waters, naturally fermented beverages like kombucha and kefir, delicious organic herbal teas and coffee, and of course, good ole' plain filtered water.

Sugar always has been one of my temptations, especially in the form of cookies, cakes, and other baked goods. I have always loved to bake, and I actually have a home-based bakery. In the old days, I would have no problem eating a couple of slices of cake or pie in a sitting, but now I try to eat more fruit instead of refined sugar. Also, I switch between raw honey and real stevia as a sweetener. Occasionally, I like to use Rapadura - a whole cane unrefined and unprocessed sugar, or organic coconut sugar in baked goods.

Step Three: Eat Organic and Grow Your Own Food

Make every attempt to consume organic food products. Get familiar with the vendors at your local farmer's markets and health food stores around town. Buy in bulk, dispense into small packages, and freeze until you need to use it. Learn what you can use from your backyard. Do you have fruit trees? What about the weeds in your yard? Did you know that some of them may be edible? Check with your local gardener's co-op extension or nursery to positively identify the plants in your yard that may be useful to you.

Plant an herb garden, even if it is an herb container in the kitchen. Start small and add more herbs as you get used to caring for them. Then, if you are up for it, start composting your vegetable and fruit scraps. One of the best ways to reintroduce minerals and nutrients into our soil is by composting scraps and adding them to your soil. When maintaining your garden, avoid using toxic poisons and weed killers, especially since you'll be eating your delicious yields.

Here are some fun dishes to try with your home-grown foods: Try fermenting vegetables and making sourdough bread. These are both super easy to do and incredible boosters for the gut. What I have found is that setting a date to get together with friends once a month to prepare these products is not only a time-saver, but it lends accountability and is a great way to spend some quality time together!

Step Four: Evaluate Your Beauty and Body Care Products

It's time to consider a new beauty routine where skin health and beauty come from the inside out. A good place to start is by choosing a healthier diet. Our skin is the largest organ on our body as a part of the integumentary system. Chemicals (also known as "ingredients") put on the skin can be absorbed through the epidermis and into the blood. Additionally, there is a possibility that when chemicals are combined, as they are in most beauty products, they have a chance of getting through the skin's protective barriers.

Take a look at the ingredient list on your favorite body lotion, and you may be overwhelmed with the lengthy list of ingredients. So, when it comes to skin and body care, my litmus test is this: If it is not safe enough to actually eat, then I don't want to put it on my skin. The same also applies to dental care products and deodorants. Perfumes are also major offenders when it comes to toxic ingredients.

Using makeup and body care products with fewer toxins should be crucial to our everyday routines. Men, try using less toxic face soaps, shave and face creams. Ladies, what about not using makeup at all? Or maybe only for work and special occasions? If you feel like you want to wear makeup every day — I know I can't be seen without my lipstick — look into using organically produced color or try some of the new beauty products made with fewer toxic ingredients.

Step Five: Know What's in Your Hair and Nail Color

When it comes to hair color, I have yet to find anything besides henna that does not use some kind of potent ingredient to maintain color. It is important to be cautious because even brands that claim not to use a certain well-known toxic ingredient may be substituting it for some lesser-known and even more harmful ingredient. The perilous aspect of hair dye is that the chemicals can pass straight into the bloodstream from the scalp. While it can affect all people, studies have found that African American and Caucasian women may be more at risk for breast cancer due to the subsequent use of hair color.[4]

I say, go gray and love it! I'm doing that, and I love never having to worry about making hair color appointments, roots showing, or spending an arm and a leg to stay on track with color. It's a blessing to be the real me and to see how time has changed me. Have you thought about doing this but feel nervous or self-conscious about it? There are support groups on Facebook and other social media for ladies who are thinking about going gray.

Nail polish is another toxic beauty product. Most common nail polishes include toluene, formaldehyde, and dibutyl phthalate chemicals, all of which are known to cause harm to the central nervous system and organ problems, and are carcinogens classified at a high danger level. Nail polish removers are equally toxic. These chemicals can enter the body through the cuticle and into the bloodstream.[5]

Consider wearing nail polish only for special occasions or not all. Give your toenails a break during the winter when you are mostly wearing closed-toed shoes. Look for less toxic polish and polish removers. Skip the extras like nail conditioners and topcoats. One of the best ways to have healthy nails is to have a healthy diet. Foods that contain iron, collagen, biotin, calcium, selenium, and zinc are all important for strong nails. To make unpainted nails look shiny, try rubbing on organic olive or coconut oil and then buff with a soft cotton cloth.

Step Six: Change Your Feminine Hygiene Products

For ladies, consider stepping away from traditional bleached feminine products and tampons made with toxic chemicals, and start using organic pads or handmade feminine napkins. The reason this is so important is that the delicate skin of the woman's vagina is much more susceptible to absorption of toxins, especially when used frequently or even daily. For a more natural and cheaper alternative, make your daily liners by cutting pieces of 100% unbleached cotton fabric which can then be laundered after use.

Step Seven: Get Out into Nature

The CDC says, "Spending time outdoors can improve overall health and wellness. The outdoors offers many opportunities to be physically active. Time outdoors may also promote mental health and stress reduction," and I certainly agree! Take a quick walk at noon to soak up some Vitamin D and get a breath of fresh air. Hiking and walking are weight-bearing exercises for the body and can be a great mental break during a busy and stressful day. Plus, you can connect with nature while building muscle and losing fat. Connecting with nature is so important that scientists have done dozens of studies hypothesizing that humans are genetically predisposed to seek connection with nature, so let's follow the science and get outside!

Step Eight: Take a Break from Technology and Wi-Fi

Unfortunately, the convenience of the internet may be costly to our health. We are more exposed to electromagnetic fields (EMFs) now than at any time in history. More studies are emerging finding that exposure to low-frequency EMFs can be related to a variety of health issues including cancer.[6] While it may seem unavoidable in this day of smartphones and free WiFi, you can attempt to shield yourself from its harmful effects.

Use headsets, speakerphone, and text rather than holding a cell phone to your head for long periods. If possible, run DSL or cable in your home for your desktop computers and reduce WiFi use as much as possible. Babies and children are especially susceptible to harmful effects; babies should never play with a cell phone or tablet. Children should be extremely limited with their use of WiFi and cell phones. So, although many aspects of the new 5G and other technology are interesting and convenient, please learn more about how it can affect your health and how to protect yourself.

While you are disconnecting from technology, why not start connecting with the earth? Grounding (or earthing) is one way to soak up the healthy and healing radiation from the earth. Try spending at least 30 minutes barefoot on a clean area of earth and enjoy the relaxing feeling you experience!

Step Nine: Give Yourself a Rest

When I was younger, I never realized how detrimental it was to be running on empty all of the time. A big family, multiple activities, and running a business all at the same time took a toll on me physically, mentally, and spiritually. The most widely read book in history, The Bible, states that we should take our day of rest, known in Hebrew as the Sabbath. A definition of "sabbath" is "to cease; to stop what we are doing and delight in that rest that was made for human beings."

I figure that if the Creator is telling us to rest, it is because we were designed to need that time to refresh ourselves to keep moving forward productively. The human body needs to rest every night for the digestive, lymphatic, and excretory systems to cleanse, heal themselves and recharge. That's also why proper sleep is so important. Our cultural expectation of a busy life can lead us to think we have no time for rest or feel guilty if we do rest. Yet, what a difference it can make when we make at least one day of rest a priority!

Step Ten: Prioritize Spending Time with Family and Dear Friends

This tip may be the last, but certainly not the least! A natural, fulfilling, and healthy life is best enjoyed with the people you care about and laugh with. Laughter is proven to increase your immunity and strengthen mental health. It can bond and connect you with others and reduce stress response levels, which is healthy for your heart.[7] Additionally, studies have also shown that physical human connection helps bolster the immune system.

And my special bonus tip for living naturally? Eat more dark chocolate! Dark chocolate has been found to include antioxidants and flavonoids that may improve heart health, cholesterol, and blood pressure levels, and may even fight cancer cells, particularly colon cancer. It also contains high amounts of nutrients including fiber, iron, magnesium, manganese, and copper.[8] You just need a little bit, and please be sure that the chocolate you eat is free of genetically modified organisms (GMOs). Your best choice will be organic and fair-trade certified.

It was my pleasure to share these tips with you on how to live a more natural, toxin-free lifestyle! Now, I'd like to challenge you to consider trying some of these ideas if you have not already. You can find details on these topics and more at my blog at **BeckyBarrancaLivingNaturally.com**.

Please share with me what aspects of your life you have changed to live more naturally. Look for the link to my healthy and simple meal plan called, "On Purpose." It's my free gift to you when you sign up for my mailing list. I look forward to it being a go-to natural living resource for you. Perhaps my experience can help you make choices that may prevent health issues for yourself and your family.

Cheers to living life naturally!

**Important note:* These products and ideas mentioned in this chapter are purely informational and not intended to diagnose, treat, cure, or prevent any disease. The author is not a medical professional and this article is not a substitute for professional care. Always consult your medical doctor regarding your health care and your use of the ideas/items mentioned in this chapter in regards to your health care status. Never disregard professional medical advice because of something you have read in this chapter.*

PUT IT INTO PRACTICE
14 Days to a More Natural Life Challenge

Day One:
Swap out your conventional dishwashing liquid with an organic version.

Day Two:
Cook today's meals from cast-iron, stainless steel, ceramic, or glass cookware, avoiding chemical-based nonstick cookware.

Day Three:
Use a diffuser with 100% pure essential oil to make your home smell good.

Day Four:
Instead of plastic bags, opt for a reusable bag to carry in your grocery haul.

Day Five:
Use a water filter to drink pure water and cut down on the use of disposable plastic bottles.

Day Six:
Brush your teeth with a natural toothpaste brand.

Day Seven:
Add two cups of Epsom salt to your bath for a detoxing soak.

Day Eight:
Swap out your shampoo and conditioner for toxin-free options.

Day Nine:
Add a few plants to your living space to improve the quality and cleanliness of the air in your home.

Day Ten:
Try making your favorite recipe using organic ingredients.

Day Eleven:
Instead of indulging a sugar craving, try a glass of water with a spritz of lemon and a 10-minute active break to beat stress.

Day Twelve:
Opt for electronic store receipts to avoid BPA-laden receipt paper.

Day Thirteen:
Instead of an energy drink, reach for an organic cup of coffee or green tea.

Day Fourteen:
Substitute your dryer sheets for reusable wool dryer balls.

Download exercise from the "Resources for Readers" section, password "Reader" at PlatformforPurposeBook.com.

Part II
Your Business

ON PURPOSE / 12 Strategies to Reclaim Your Power and Change Your Life

Learn About
Dr. Erika Brown

Dr. Erika Brown is the CEO of Dr. Erika By Design. In her late 30s, she suffered what some would refer to as a quarter-life crisis. She was unfulfilled in her job, her health was declining, and her mojo was a "no-go." At that point she felt that life had to be more than just working in corporate America. So, she decided to change her mindset and focus on finding her way back to the Erika she once knew long ago.

As a result, she found herself on this crazy, bumpy, exhilarating ride called entrepreneurship. In a matter of six months, she changed career paths, started an internationally recognized podcast, became an author, and began to work with some amazing clients.

Through her work as a coach, consultant, and podcast host, Dr. Erika is working to fulfill her purpose of helping high-achieving women share their story, build their dreams, and execute their vision.

Connect with Dr. Erika Brown
Website: DrErikabyDesign.com
Email: DrErika@DrErikabyDesign.com

Chapter Seven

Breaking Patterns of Chaos that Stifle Your Productivity

by Dr. Erika Brown

Have you ever experienced a day when you fell down the "time" rabbit hole? You know those days where it seems like everything takes too long, nothing gets accomplished, and time moves at the speed of lightning. Let me paint a picture for you of what a typical day might look like when you've gotten lost in the rabbit hole:

Today I am on a mission! I am determined to be out of the office by 5 p.m. sharp. No staying late like I typically do. It's 9 a.m. and I'm ready to start my day. First, I'll sketch out the vision for my business. I have my post-its, my markers, and my highlighters. I have big goals! But I also know I need to work on getting clients, so I jump to that task, starting to work on my new consulting client workflow. I've heard about this amazing tool that can help me with email marketing, so I head over to the Dubsado website, and, after two hours of playing around in the system, I'm more lost than before I started. Is it already lunch time? Let's just put that task off until tomorrow.

Maybe I should get back to planning out my vision. While I'm flipping through the pages of my journal for inspiration, I run across a note to myself about purchasing a pop filter for my microphone. This filter will definitely help me step up my podcasting game. So, I head over to Amazon to do some research. Then I remember that I need to grab that new book on effective marketing that a fellow coach talked about on Clubhouse.

Now, who was it that told me about that book? Oh yeah, I remember. Wait, she was supposed to go live on Instagram today. Let me head over there and see if I can catch.

Wait, what was I supposed to be doing? It's already 4 p.m. And I'm exhausted. The day just flew by, and I still have so much work left to do. I'll never be able to leave the office at 5 p.m. I guess I should brew another cup of coffee. It's going to be an all-nighter again. I swear I need more hours in my day.

Sound familiar? Yep, I get it! I have seen this rabbit hole sabotage many entrepreneurs.

In fact, this rabbit hole has been the cause of many of my clients experiencing an abundance of overwhelm, an endless feeling of being scattered, and the inability to execute goals. My clients are high-achieving, ambitious, and highly successful women. However, for most of them, that success has not come without long nights, declining health, and failing relationships. They have dedicated their lives to being the best, but at an extremely high cost. Often, they trade dollars for health and coins for time they will never get back. They fall into the trap of thinking things can never change and that life and business will always be a whirlwind of half-finished projects, piles of sticky notes, and gallons of caffeine.

Is this striking a chord? Don't fret! There is hope.
In working with clients, I have found that there are patterns of chaos that can inhibit your success if they go unrecognized. These patterns impact your productivity, organization, and efficiency. They can be masked by good intention and progress, but when you start to unwrap the

layers, you unmask the root cause of the struggle.
In my business, I typically encounter four personality types that are associated with specific patterns of chaos:

- The Visionary
- The Superwoman
- The Squirrel
- The Perfect Planner

Each personality can be tied to a lack in certain foundations of productivity. The Visionary lacks action steps. The Superwoman lacks boundaries. The Squirrel lacks focus. The Perfect Planner lacks flexibility. As a result, each personality experiences what I refer to as "stifled success." This occurs when the true level of your success is being stifled due to lack.

How would it feel to break the patterns of chaos and escape from that "stifled success"? How much more successful would you be if you recognized these areas of lack and understood your productivity personality? How much more could you contribute to the world if you got a handle on your time? How much more impact could you make if you stopped stifling your own success?

Identify Your Pattern

It's time to buckle up, Buttercup, because now is the opportunity for you to dig deep and finally understand why you've struggled to move forward. By the end of this chapter, you'll identify your typical personality type and learn strategies to push through the patterns of chaos impeding your business and personal success.

THE VISIONARY

The Visionary has ideas of grandeur floating through her head, even as she sleeps. Her desk is likely covered with colorful sticky notes and her office likely plastered with white boards often filled with notes. The Visionary is an innovator and thrives on being a multi-talented and multi-passionate individual. Time for brainstorming and mind-mapping are definitely priorities. The Visionary is great at setting big, audacious goals but never quite executes a sustainable action plan. Imagine if Michelangelo proudly pronounced that he was going to paint the ceiling of the Sistine Chapel, but he never took the time to get the paint, failed to consider how long the project would take or how he would reach the ceiling to create the masterpiece. Having a vision is only the first step. A vision without action is merely a dream.

Tips for Visionaries:

Create an action plan. Take time to think about your goals. Are they realistic? If the answer is yes, then do a brain dump. List all the action steps necessary to achieve that goal. Prioritize the list, assign deadlines, and assign responsibilities.

Use daily themes. As a multi-passionate individual, you have several projects on your plate. Assign each day a theme that correlates to your projects or type of work. For example, Monday's theme is podcasting. Tuesday's theme is client work. Wednesday is for deep focus work. You get to decide how you want to break up your week. Don't worry. It's not set in stone. Keep in mind that this is just a guidepost to your day. You may do other tasks throughout the day, but the themes are your focus.

Planned white space. Visionaries need time for visualizing. So give yourself some white space on your calendar. Plan breaks throughout the day. Allow your mind time to unwind and flow.

THE SUPERWOMAN

The Superwoman is likely to be smiling on the outside but stressed on the inside. The Superwoman has spent her life jumping over obstacles in a single bound, fighting the good fight against mediocrity, failure, and negative opinions. However, she often finds herself exhausted, frustrated, and confused. The Superwoman piles on task after task because she says yes out of obligation. She tackles project upon project, thinking that she alone must do everything.

> **Having a vision is only the first step. A vision without action is merely a dream.**

The Superwoman will stretch herself paper thin and take on new opportunity upon new opportunity in an attempt to avoid FOMO (fear of missing out). However, in trying to do everything, she is accomplishing nothing.

Tips for Superwomen:

Embrace delegation. It's time to spread the love. Identify tasks and projects that can be delegated to others. Ask yourself these questions:

- Do I want to do this task?
- Are there others that can do this task more efficiently than me?
- How much time would it take me to complete this task?
- What type of return on investment (ROI) do I get for completing this task myself?

Get analytical about new opportunities. It's great to have new opportunities coming to your door or email, but you only have twenty-four hours in a day and twelve months in a year. Your business is important, but so is family time, social time, and the other many facets of your life. So, before you say yes, be sure to analyze the opportunity. These questions will help:

- Is this something that you are excited about doing?
- Does it align with your business and life goals?
- Do you have the time capacity to not only engage in the opportunity but also effectively prepare?

Automate your life. While delegation involves a handoff to an actual person or team, automation involves setting up systems for things that consume your precious time. Automate tasks that are repetitive and tasks that need to be consistent.

THE SQUIRREL

The Squirrel is often thrown off by shiny-object-syndrome. Although the Squirrel starts the day with plans of completing a task, something pops into her brain that completely destroys that focus. It could be something as simple as a phone call that lasts just a little too long. Or something that takes her down a social media spiral for hours. It doesn't matter what the distraction is because in that moment, this new "shiny object" has taken precedence.

The Squirrel struggles with long periods of focus and needs variety in her day. In addition, sitting in the office at the desk for hours is not an option for the Squirrel. Asking the Squirrel to focus on a project for three hours is not going to work. As a result, instead of being productive, she is now trapped in the storm of "busy"ness.

Tips for the Squirrel:

Tools are your friend. We live in a world where technology is able to help us do just about anything. In fact, there are tools available to help you focus. Here are some ideas:

- Try different apps that are designed to measure your focus.
- Go old school and call a friend. Create virtual focus sessions and hold each other accountable.
- Try my favorite: Find your most productive space. I believe we all have certain spaces that produce various levels of focus. Identify the places that result in the greatest focus for your task and start to use those locations for that type of work only.

Be a sprinter. There is no rule that says you must lock yourself in a room and work on a project for hours at a time until it's finished. Instead, try to break up your tasks into small blocks of time. A great tool that works for many people is the Pomodoro method. This method lets you give your full focus for twenty minutes, then you take a five-minute break, and then you repeat it all over again. Be sure to use a timer to stay on track.

Use distractions as rewards. Distractions are inevitable, but what if you could use them as motivation? Let's say going on Amazon and swiping through Instagram are your typical distractions. Make a deal with yourself. Write it down if you have to: "When I complete XYZ, then I will allow myself to XYZ for X number of minutes." In this scenario, once you complete your tasks, you will allow yourself to scroll on Instagram for ten minutes. Basically, you decided to withhold yourself from the distraction until you have completed the tasks.

THE PERFECT PLANNER

Detail-oriented and organized are two words that describe the Perfect Planner. The Perfect Planner's pattern of chaos is often not obvious. Her chaos arises from the need for everything and anything be perfect. She must perfect every detail of every project before it sees the light of day. She needs her day to go exactly as planned because she has meticulously scheduled every moment with care and precision. She is data-driven and will research "till the cows come home" to ensure that she is doing, saying, or presenting the "right" thing. For the Perfect Planner, deadlines are not optional; they are a part of life.

Tips for Perfect Planners:

Choose progress over perfection. Sometimes procrastination masquerades as perfectionism. Instead of holding on to the stress, confusion, and fear of something not being perfect, begin to embrace that progress is still possible. Understand that nothing will ever be perfect; however, you cannot improve upon something that has not been set free.

Reject information hoarding. Research can provide much needed data and insight, but it can also be a crutch. Instead of diving into a research frenzy, evaluate the project or task:

- What information do you truly need to know?
- How will this information move the project forward?
- And the extra credit question: How much time will I dedicate to this research? That's right. Give yourself a time limit so you can focus on the true needs at the moment and not the extra fluff that you may find along the way.

Work on your mind. In the world of the Perfect Planner,

a lot of the challenges start internally. You ask yourself questions: Is this enough? Is there value? What if it's not right? Those are all questions that play on repeat in the mind of the Perfect Planner. Give yourself an anti-perfectionism shower daily. Wash yourself in words of affirmation. Remind yourself of your past successes. Remember that you have accomplished so much in the past and today's goals and dreams will be no different.

Next Steps

Do you remember that old cartoon, Popeye the Sailor Man? Every episode, you would hear Popeye proclaim, "I yam what I yam an' tha's all I yam." Many people still believe this old adage. They believe that they are not capable of change. Believe that the person they are today can't grow to be more tomorrow. Believe that their weaknesses define them more than their strengths. But what if that's all a fallacy? You do not have to stay trapped, allowing your patterns of chaos to define you.

Although patterns of chaos can be difficult to break, they don't have to define you, nor do they have to impede your progress. Unlike Popeye, you are capable of change. You can identify resources, tools, and people that can help you.

The bottom-line: You don't have to stay stagnant. After reading this chapter and doing some self-inventory, you now understand your productivity personality and your patterns.

The great news is that you can begin to implement the tips we discussed in your life and start to see immediate impacts on your business and your life.

And let me set someone free right now — Perfect Planners, I need you to read this statement twice! When you start working on these patterns and implementing these techniques, the result is not going to be perfect. Understand that productivity, efficiency, and balance are an art, not an exact science. You need to find the strategies that work for you and the tips that fit into your life (don't try to force it).

> **No matter how good you are at one thing, there is always some other area of life or business that you struggle in.**

I have given you several tools for your toolbox, and now it's time for you to create your own personalized prescription for enhancing your productivity, for improving your time-management, and for corralling your chaos.

So, what's next for you? For some, these few pages of insta-coaching may be enough. You may come back to this chapter from time to time and refer to these tips over the next few days.

But what happens in the next few weeks, the next few months? Let's be honest. If you could handle all the chaos that keeps you stagnant on your own, you wouldn't be this far along in this chapter. You need more than your own willpower; you need help. You need accountability. You need someone who will walk with you on this journey. Truth be told, we all need help from time to time. No matter how good you are at one thing, there is always some other area of life or business that you struggle in.

Asking for help, however, does not come natural to us high achievers. Even when you have the strength to ask for help, subsequent challenges come to mind — what type of help do you need and how do you find it? Being a high achieving businesswoman or entrepreneur requires a delicate balance of trust and confidence. Trust in your own abilities as a boss and confidence in the skills of those you bring along for the ride. Confidence in the tribe you build around you. Confidence in the team you create to help you break through these patterns of chaos.

I know some of you are probably rolling your eyes at me right now. But how many times have you stopped yourself from asking for help because you felt as though you could wear all the hats and do all the things?

How many times have you imagined where your business would be, if only? If only you had a team? If only you were more organized? If only you could find more time in your day to be in your true zone of genius?

Now that you recognize your patterns, you understand what's lacking, and you realize how it's hurting your business, what's next? How are you going to fix the problem? How will you escape the pattern of chaos in your life? It's time to be honest with yourself. You know you can't do it alone. It's time to get support.

If you are tired of having your patterns of chaos run you, then I invite you to connect with me. Schedule your free clarity call to talk about the challenges and struggles you have. Together we can change the trajectory of your business and your life so that you are no longer frustrated and frazzled, but instead you design a life where you are productive, peaceful, and profitable.

Schedule your clarity call at **www.talkwithdrerika.com**.

PUT IT INTO PRACTICE
Recommended Resources

Looking for resources to help you boost your productivity? I've handpicked a few of my favorites to help address your pattern of chaos. These are guaranteed to score you some quick productivity wins!

ClickUp (Project Management Tool): With ClickUp, you can assign tasks to your team, track their progress, and hit your goals without flying solo.

Dubsado (Client Management and Workflow System): Dubsado makes it easy to create workflows, invoice clients, and streamline your correspondence to clients, collaborators, and vendors.

Atomic Habits (Book): Learn the art of creating good habits and eliminating bad habits from author James Clear.

My Free Resources Available at www.DrErikaFreeGift.com:

Creating Clarity and Capacity in Life and Business: 28 Day Challenge Guide
28 easy tactics to create more clarity in your day and help you make the most of your time.

10 Favorite Organization and Time Management Tools
Get 10 of my favorite tools that keep me from swimming in overwhelm.

Dr. Erika by Design Podcast (YouTube)
Learn about the journeys of women entrepreneurs from all backgrounds as well as tips and tricks on creating success and being organized.

Download exercise from the "Resources for Readers" section, password "Reader" at PlatformforPurposeBook.com.

Learn About
Connie Vanderzanden

Connie Vanderzanden is on a mission to help entrepreneurs live the lifestyles they desire by learning the simple steps, structure, and discipline to create and save money.

With 34 years of accounting and bookkeeping experience, a variety of industry knowledge, and her own real-life business growth journey since 2001, Connie developed the Going Beyond Revenue Cash Handling System, focused on cash flow planning that creates profitable and sustainable businesses.

Connie is a true Oregonian, born and raised in the beautiful Pacific Northwest where she spends time with her husband of 34 years and their "fur kid."

Connect with Connie Vanderzanden
Website: ProfitwithConnie.com
Email: Connie@ProfitwithConnie.com

Chapter Nine

Your Best Team Member: Money

by Connie Vanderzanden

Back in 2000 when I decided to scale my business, the idea of creating a team was a little daunting. So much so that I took some time to gather support from trusted business coaches and HR Specialists for the first hiring round and then again to help with team communication and bonding. It was an interesting journey that left me juggling the tasks of managing my staff, delegating work assignments, and flatout dodging my responsibilities as the "boss" — secretly hoping and wishing that my dream team would form from thin-air and magically deliver the results to my doorstep.

Looking back on this chaotic hiring process, I can see now that there was one key team member I failed to acknowledge. While this team member didn't possess a physical body like my other team members, this staff member was very present in my daily interactions. This employee works for every entrepreneur and is the key player that forms our decisions and fuels our passion and desires for our businesses. Who is it?

It's Money.

Here's what a typical workday may look like in your

business with Money: You'll find Money collaborating with you on a sales call. It shows up in your bank account as a client payment. Money supports you and the business as you pay yourself and then your team. This employee silently cheers you on from its office, your company's savings account.

When you treat Money with respect, it provides you with an invisible energetic support system. When you have more gratitude for how Money does its job, you naturally have more joy and spend your day looking up for all the abundance and opportunities that are presenting themselves. When Money feels it's a valued member of the team, it will naturally attract more of itself.

What happens when you don't value your employee, Money? Neglecting Money by paying bills late, brings negative and costly consequences such as incurring late fees. Ignoring Money can lead to forgetting to invoice clients, and slowing the payment process down. When you ignore Money's contributions, you end up focusing only on what is lacking. This often manifests as slowly increasing debt and cash shortages.

Let me be the first to confess that I've ignored this essential team member for many years. I learned the hard way the importance of creating a nurturing relationship with Money. I don't want you to experience the same pitfalls I did, but instead learn from my mistakes as you start treating Money like you would your best team member. Let me show you how and why this strategy works.

All team members, whether they work onsite or remotely, look to you to provide three key things: **Consistency, Structure** and **Gratitude.** Money is no different.

CREATING CONSISTENCY WITH MONEY

Team members thrive on consistency. Knowing what to expect, when it will happen, and how they will deliver the work is key. Trust me, if you constantly change the process or the game plan every time the team comes in, they will not stay very long. While you the entrepreneur may be flexible and in the creative flow, you hire team members to be in their strengths which is normally the "doing" of the tasks that you are not fabulous at.

Money is no different. Here are four ways you can create and foster an environment of consistency in your business when working with Money:

1. **Get Clear on Your Expectations and Needs with Money**
   Before starting the hiring process, we first envision what needs to be done. Be aware that not all the answers will be easy to identify in the initial planning stages. Those will come later, so regular planning sessions are required to make sure you stay on track.

   For Money, setting clear expectations means crafting a financial plan, a map of where you are today and where you want to go. Create a budget, citing every service, tool, and employee necessary then assign a dollar value to each item. The financial plan is the blueprint of what Money will be creating.

2. **Check-in with Your Employee, Money**
   Nothing is worse for a team than neglecting weekly check-ins and failing to follow-up on assigned tasks. Without accountability, teams get off track, which in turns frustrates management (aka us business owners). This leads to hurt feelings and team turnover. You can avoid this unwanted drama by having regular weekly check-in meetings. As managers, we encourage employees to stay on-top of tasks by asking them what's going on this week, what happened last week,

what worked and what didn't. The same must be done with Money.

Check-in with Money by bookkeeping each week. I call this process, "Money Monday." Using an automated tool such as QuickBooks Online, I keep the updates quick and easy. (This software works for me, but I encourage you to find what works best for your company.)
By carefully reflecting on Money's activity, I'm able to evaluate questions such as: Did all the money I expected come in last week? What didn't work well? Doing this has helped me catch problems such as tight cash flows and unpaid vendors. Examine the data to discover what support is needed; then consider what support you can take on and what should be delegated.

Finally, I want to remind you that there's a fine line between obsessing over and paying attention to Money. By practicing a weekly check-in and creating a pause in the spending process, you keep your finger on the pulse of what is going on without checking your bank balance multiple times throughout your day.

3. **Ensure that Money Shows Up and Delivers Results**
After all the research, planning, and discussion happens, we must take action. What does action look like for Money? I am talking about inviting others to work with you and asking for the sale.

With Money, you'll want to be sure that each of its assignments is revenue-generating. If we want Money to be present and productive, we must talk to people and ask for it. We can't hide away in our offices doing busy work and neglect having a sales conversation, networking, or connecting with other like-minded business owners and expect Money to simply fall from the sky.

Yes, abundance is all around us and what we truly desire already exists. The Universe will energetically align the ideal people to knock on our doors or connect us with the people ready to take action. However, If we don't answer the door and tell people about what we do, and more importantly ASK them if they want to work with us, money won't show up. You must take action to support Money in its role.

4. **Create a Pause in Money's Process**
   This is one thing that is specific to your relationship with Money. Rather than outflow happening immediately, create a pause in the process. Allow Money to settle. Take a breath... a beat. Then ask Money to get to work.

   When you shift from being reactive around requests for Money to having a process and plan, it allows you to uphold boundaries between the business and Money. This one shift in how you interact with Money may be the most empowering action you take for the business and ultimately, yourself.

Consistency leads us to creating structure. While consistency focuses on setting the intention of how Money will support your business, creating a structure allows us to set boundaries around how Money flows in and out. In fact, as you were considering what consistency would look like, you already got a glimpse of the system and structure you will use for this next step.

CREATING STRUCTURE FOR MONEY

As solo-preneurs we often lack systems to accomplish routine tasks, which won't fly when scaling our team. Whether it's on paper or in a project management system, we must document our processes. This enables new employees to quickly take action, communicate clearly, and effectively serve within their role in moving your business forward. While Money may not verbally provide feedback or insights, documenting this process will allow you to identify problem-areas and bring more stability to your business. Here are some practical ways to consider creating structure for Money:

Create Boundaries with Money
Working with a remote team? You don't make yourself available based on their availability, you hire based on them being available for YOU! This is a little shout-out to the Universe at large. By crafting the plan and checking in weekly, you know what amounts of cash flow needs to shift by and when.

Now it's time to speak up and make a verbal request. Best results happen when you use your outside voice, rather than simply thinking about the number. By leaning into the abundance of the Universe, ask for a little support so it can gradually push the resources (people and time) towards you so Money can do its thing. This isn't only a hope and prayer tactic. This is voicing and tracking what is required and firmly using your faith muscle to hold that desire strong so it can be created.

Craft Money's Job Title
Job descriptions may seem old-fashioned, but they're still helpful. A single team member, depending on their strengths, may do a little bit of everything, but crafting a basic description will help everyone get started.

For Money, that means identifying what the intentional use will be and plastering that everywhere you track Money. Edit your online access so the name of the account shifts from Checking to "Owner's Pay" or "Profit." Edit the name in your accounting tool or spreadsheet. Make sure when you see a bank statement, it is clearly reflected. If it is helpful to have a little tally sheet on your desk or big ol' whiteboard, remember to use the intentional use job description.

Money feels heard and seen when you give it a title, and it loves telling people what it's intentional use is.

STOP RECREATING THE WHEEL

This is the first thing you do when you leverage your time. It's all about getting what's in your head out onto paper. It's how the team is trained to duplicate your actions, and yes, learn how to think like you would.

Having established processes for your weekly updates means that Money isn't left somewhere to be forgotten and lost. After a while, these processes become habit and it simply is how you interact with Money. If you find yourself resisting this change, consider this: Is it worth your time to recreate the wheel every time you interact with Money?

For example, one way I've seen entrepreneurs create more work for themselves is lacking solid payment processes. Each client may have a unique billing schedule. Or different team members are paid at different times, in multiple ways. Can you see how this lack of consistency introduces confusion and hinders you from receiving timely payments?

Take control of when the payment comes in by setting up recurring and automated direct bank payments. Add deadlines to your invoices to ensure that clients make payments promptly to avoid penalties. Or bill retainers to cover the current month's services and team costs, rather than billing after the work is complete.

Let's ditch the mental gymnastics it takes to manage our structures in our heads. I encourage you to take advantage of the countless project management software tools currently available. Otherwise, you'll miss out on the opportunities to improve and multiply your Money's efforts. Seeing Money's positive impact on your business will definitely move you to gratitude, which is the next item on our agenda.

PRACTICING GRATITUDE FOR MONEY

Finally, **gratitude** is the secret success sauce to any great long-term team. Regular feedback to team members is helpful, but showing them a little love and gratitude goes a long way when it comes to building a team.

Speak Money's Love Language
One way is to express your gratitude to an employee is to figure out what their love language is or what values they lead with. For example, a team member that has a strong value around family will appreciate a paid day off over a gift card. Or knowing that a team member loves gifts, a small token of appreciation will make them feel unique and special.

Money's love language is words of appreciation. You can do this by identifying daily why you are grateful for Money and how it adds to you and your business lives. Start the day identifying the intention and Universal request of the best way Money can support you. As you wrap for the day, take a quick moment to identify one thing that you are grateful about when it comes to Money.

How will you change your relationship with Money? What items above seemed easy to incorporate and which ones are you curious about, but not sure how to execute them?

TAKE ACTION

Before we end our time together, I want to leave you with this quote from Barbara Huson: *"When you treat money with the reverence and respect it deserves, it will shower endless blessings upon you, allowing you to serve others for all your days and beyond."*

Now is the time to nurture and empower your best team member, Money. As it grows, so will the resources that help you reach your goals, allowing you to make a bigger impact, and be the difference you want to see in the world.

If you found this chapter insightful, I invite you to connect with me for a complimentary 30-minute conversation about Money, your business, and what you would like to create with them both. Get started by visiting
MeetWithConnie.com.

PUT IT INTO PRACTICE
Manifest Your Big Dream

Let us not forget that the reason behind building a financially thriving business is to manifest your big dream. Your big dream is that secret overall goal for our life or business. It's that grand idea and desire that was downloaded from Spirit and it is your purpose in this lifetime to start creating.

This is where the energy of Money comes in. Remember, it's not about being perfect and you don't have to know all the answers.

Mental Rehearsal Exercise
Take a moment to meditate or use your breath to move from being all caught up in your mind and move into a more grounded space solidly in your body.

Now pause.

In this very grounded space, you are going to have a conversation with your business. If you've never considered your business as a separate entity, just go with it — it may actually be one of the most empowering conversations you have.

Do your best to tap into your intuition, listen to that inner voice for the answer and ask the louder annoying Ego voice to take a back seat. When negativity starts filtering in, breathe and recenter yourself.

Create the most vivid details possible. Pay attention to what you are wearing, the environment, who is with you, what you smell, taste, or hear. Then, take time to settle into the feelings.

HERE ARE SOME QUESTIONS TO ASK YOUR BUSINESS:
- What is its big vision?
- What does your business ultimately want to create as its legacy?
- What impact does it want to make?
- Do you want to impact one person, one hundred, one thousand, more?
- What people or causes will you financially support through your business?
- Can you imagine what your team would look like?
- Where might your "office" be?
- Ask your business and Spirit team if there is anything else about this vision you need to know.

_____
_____
_____
_____
_____
_____
_____
_____
_____
_____

Download exercise from the "Resources for Readers" section, password "Reader" at PlatformforPurposeBook.com.

ON PURPOSE / 12 Strategies to Reclaim Your Power and Change Your Life

Learn About
Isha Cogborn

Isha Cogborn is the founder of Epiphany Institute, where she helps people connect their purpose and passion to their profession.

As a nationally sought-ought speaker, three-time author and podcast host, Isha couples two decades of experience helping corporations and individuals make a greater impact with the resilience birthed from being a teenage mother on welfare, corporate layoffs and a bout with homelessness after a failed business venture. In 2017, Isha also founded Startup Life Support to help entrepreneurs overcome the fear, overwhelm and isolation of starting a business.

Isha earned a degree in Broadcast & Cinematic Arts from Central Michigan University and is member of Alpha Kappa Alpha Sorority, Inc. The Michigan native now lives in the Phoenix area, where she enjoys Netflix binges and Peloton rides.

Connect with Isha Cogborn:
Website: EpiphanyInstitute.com
Email: Isha@EpiphanyInstitute.com

Chapter Ten

Platform for Purpose: How to Grow Your Audience and Your Impact

by Isha Cogborn

Since I was 14 years old, I knew that I wanted to share information that would change people's lives and inspire them to be better versions of themselves. I wanted to have a platform for people who were doing good in the world so that their impact could be even greater.

Charting a career today with that mission might seem like a no-brainer thanks to social media, self-publishing and the ability to create an internationally-known personal brand with your mobile phone. But back then, the only path that seemed to make sense was becoming a journalist.

After earning a degree in broadcast journalism, I discovered a startling fact: I hated news. Maybe *hate* is a strong word. And I didn't dislike all news, just the depressing stuff. I knew my sensitive spirit couldn't handle covering tragedy and mayhem day in and day out. Instead, I ended up in corporate communications where I actually got an opportunity to host and produce a TV show and global broadcasts for a chemical company. Imagine that! But the higher I ascended on the corporate ladder, the further away I got from the work I loved.

After getting laid off in 2009, I founded Epiphany Institute, a professional development company that helps people connect their purpose and passions with their profession. I discovered that new options existed to create the profession I dreamed about as a teenager. When I realized I could forge a path not limited to the bullet points of a corporate job description, I wanted to shout it from the mountaintops so everyone would know they had options, too!

I also discovered that I could now reach people without the gatekeepers of traditional media. In the years to come, I launched a blog, started my own podcast and self-published books (including the one you're reading now). Not once did I ask for anyone's permission or jump through hoops to prove that I was worthy of sharing my message.

But as the tools get easier to use and more people jump into the fray, it's becoming harder to capture meaningful attention. Social media platforms like Facebook, Instagram and LinkedIn use ever-changing algorithms to serve up the most popular content to users. The more people who engage with your content, the more it shows up in timelines and newsfeeds. Content creators who used to enjoy major traction are now relying on sponsored posts to hit the same numbers.

RISE OF THE INFLUENCERS

The early 2000's ushered in a wave of celebrities like Paris Hilton and Kim Kardashian who were both lauded and loathed as being "famous for nothing." From reality shows to clothing lines, these personalities learned how to monetize their magnetism.

Today, this strategy isn't limited to hotel heiresses and the Hollywood elite. Regular people just like you are building personal brands that attract the attention of companies looking to cut through the noise and humanize their brands. While the focus used to be on social media users with huge followings, brands are now recognizing that quantity doesn't always mean quality when it comes to a loyal audience. An entire industry has emerged to match the right influencers with the right brands.

Influencers are 'word of mouth marketing on steroids' because they already have a following who trust their opinions. It's important to note that these tribes aren't always built because the influencer is the most knowledgeable source available but often because their personality, values or experiences create a connection with their audience.

Why Does This Matter to You?
Whether you're looking to attract brands and sponsors or just want to deliver your message more meaningfully, simply putting information out there and hoping people pay attention won't cut it anymore. You have to infuse you into your message.

Why are there hundreds of books on a single topic available on Amazon? Why has cable news viewership eclipsed local ratings? Because people crave connection, not just information. They're looking for someone who gets them.

We all have the ability to present a different take on a topic based on who we are, our life experiences and the lens through which we see the world. However, too many of us have pushed our views and personality down to our toes because someone told us we were too quirky, not polished enough or that our opinions were too polarizing.

There are people who will never like you, no matter how hard you work to win them over. Instead of focusing on them, what if you found the people who will love you just the way you are? I'm not saying you shouldn't focus on improving the way you deliver a message, but that's not the same as force-fitting yourself into someone else's box. What makes you different from other people who do what you do may be the very thing that attracts your tribe. It's the essence of your personal brand.

WHAT IS PERSONAL BRANDING?

Many oversimplify branding as logos or color schemes associated with a product or business. While visual elements may represent the brand, it goes much deeper. Here's my favorite definition of branding:

"Branding is the recognition of a personal connection that forms in the hearts and minds of customers and key audiences through their accumulated experience at every point of contact."

Although difficult to measure in dollars and cents, branding is a form of currency. A strong, positive brand fosters loyalty that keeps customers from jumping ship for competitors. Because a brand is built through accumulated experiences over time, customers are also more forgiving of errors if the bulk of their experiences have been positive.

I first became acquainted with the term "personal branding" after reading a 1997 article by Tom Peters in Fast Company magazine. Although I may not have had the terminology to explain it, I understood from an early age that I had some control over the narrative that formed in people's heads when they interacted with me. From the clothes I wore to the extracurricular clubs I joined, I made choices that aligned with the way I wanted people to see me. When I landed a co-op job at a bank at the age of 16, I wore business suits to school. People in other departments thought I was a full-time salaried employee!

Everything you do (or don't do) either strengthens or diminishes your personal brand. There was a consultant I had been watching on social media with thoughts of signing up for one of her programs. When I saw her go on a tirade about a customer, I decided to go another route. I'm sure she was just having a bad day and let her frustration get the best of her, but I hadn't had enough positive experiences with her yet to keep it from negatively impacting my opinion of her. None of us are perfect, but being deliberate about the way we show up in the world increases our chances of attracting and retaining the right audience. In case you think I'm contradicting myself from earlier in the chapter, please understand that it's not about trying to make everyone happy. It's about not unintentionally driving away the people we want to work with.

THE POWER OF A PLATFORM

Social media gives you the opportunity to communicate more broadly than ever before, but sharing your opinion doesn't mean you have a platform. At any time, you can be put into "Facebook jail" if you do something that breaks their rules because it's not YOUR platform. You are a user on THEIR platform. Building a platform means creating vehicles that you have full editorial control over (within the guidelines of the law) such as:

- Blogs
- Podcasts
- Events
- Books
- Video programming/films/documentaries
- Educational products

From social justice to sexual abuse, platforms driven by regular people are bringing a voice to the voiceless. Although unarmed African-Americans have been disproportionately killed by law enforcement since being kidnapped and brought to the US in chains, the nation didn't begin to have meaningful dialogue about the issue until #BlackLivesMatter created a platform for the conversation. dream hampton's documentary on the decades-long allegations of sexual abuse against singer R. Kelly not only led to new investigations into his behavior, but it also provided a space for communities to speak out against the ignored victimization of women at the hands of family members and acquaintances.

Platforms can organize scattered voices into a powerful force. Platforms can educate, enlighten and empower. And when platforms are driven by people that we like and trust, we can be inspired to change our lives and the world around us.

PERSONAL BRAND + PLATFORM = IMPACT

If you've built a platform, but you're struggling to gain traction, chances are, there's a disconnect between who you are, who you want to help and what you're presenting to the world. Here are five strategies to help you build a more impactful platform:

1. **Check Your Ego at the Door**
   If you're doing this just to get attention, you're in it for the wrong reason. If you're doing it to prove all of the people who didn't believe in you wrong, your motivation is shrouded in negative energy. Ask yourself, "How do I want people to be better because they came in contact with me?" It's not about you. You're the pipe that greatness flows through to positively impact the lives of others.

2. **Know Your Audience**
   One of the first questions I ask new clients is, "Who is your target audience?" If they say, "Everybody", then I know we have work to do. A key element of breaking through the noise and meaningfully connecting with your audience is knowing as much as possible about the people you want to reach. Traditionally, we've looked at demographics like

age, gender, socioeconomic status and the like. But psychographics, defined by Merriam-Webster Dictionary as "market research or statistics classifying population groups according to psychological variables (such as attitudes, values, or fears)" are much more effective.

> **Platforms can organize scattered voices into a powerful force.**

If you're looking to help people solve a problem that you've solved for yourself, your best audience may be people who were like you. What challenges did you routinely face as a result of the problem? What was your motivation to fix it? What barriers stood between you and what you desired? How did the voices in your head and the people around you affect your progress?

By understanding where your target audience is, what they want and what they need, and by routinely speaking to it, your content will make them feel like you're walking around in their head. Wouldn't you rather listen to somebody who gets you specifically instead of speaking in broad, generic terms? When you try to reach everybody, you'll have a hard time reaching anybody.

3. **Pick Your Vehicle**

   One of the greatest challenges people experience (including myself at times) is consistency. For years, my fear of inconsistency punked me out of starting a meetup group and launching a podcast. Then I realized that my 'on again, off again' ways were the consequence of biting off more than I could chew. If I didn't try to take on so much, I could be more consistent.

Many marketing gurus will tell you that you need to be everywhere — blogging, YouTube, Facebook, LinkedIn, Instagram, podcasting, speaking, networking...are you tired yet? If you're committed to getting more than four hours of sleep each night, I challenge you to choose no more than two primary vehicles where you'll "live". This is the space where you'll share valuable content and build an engaged community. It could be a meetup group, online show, monthly webinars, or anything your target audience will find valuable and where they're likely to find you based on their lifestyle and habits. Being an early adopter on the latest emerging vehicle might seem like a good idea, but if your target audience isn't there yet, make sure you focus on growing your platform elsewhere, too.

Also look to vehicles that showcase your strengths. Do you have a vibrant and engaging personality? Video and speaking may serve you well. Would you rather put the spotlight on others? Consider a podcast.

4. **Find Your Voice**
Curating content by sharing articles, videos and quotes from other experts can be an effective strategy. But if you want to be seen as a thought leader, you have to also tell your audience what you think. One of the fears that I help my clients overcome is feeling like they don't have anything new or valuable to say.

Here's a strategy to help you develop a fresh point of view:

Allow your brain to objectively process the

information you receive instead of accepting it as truth — even if it's from a respected source. Has anything from your experiences provided you with a different perspective? What is missing from the conversation? Who is missing from the conversation? Dissenting from popular opinion can be scary, but it may be just what your audience needs. How can you give a voice to the voiceless?

Adopt a tone and style that allows your personality to shine through — even if you don't think it's particularly magnetic. This should go without saying, but actually communicate like a person. Unless your target audience is academic professionals, your content doesn't have to sound like a textbook. If your tribe is simply looking for information, a Google search will suffice. The way you serve up the information is what will get their attention and keep them coming back.

5. **Embrace Imperfection.**
   As I talk to prospective collaborators for my Platform for Purpose Initiative, there are common fears and insecurities that arise:

"What if I mess up?"

"I need to lose weight before I start making videos."

"I don't like the way I look or sound on the air."

"What if I don't get my content out on schedule?"

"I don't know enough to be looked at as an expert."

"What if someone disagrees with me?"

At the root, it all comes down to an unrealistic expectation of perfection. We feel like we have to do everything right and everyone needs to like us in order to make a difference. Let me take the pressure off of you with this newsflash: You will never be perfect, and that's okay.

In a world where every post is filtered and social media feeds are carefully curated, many audiences are placing greater value on transparency and imperfection. We want to hear from people who feel accessible and make us believe we can be like them, too.

Oprah Winfrey is easily the most recognizable media personality in the world. When national syndication of her television show began in the 80's, she was making the same "trash TV" as her counterparts on other networks. But then she decided to take us on her personal journey for a better life. She invited us to read the books she read and learn from the experts who changed her life. As a result, we became better...together. She shared her pain and struggles — from being sexually abused, challenges maintaining a healthy weight, and even secrets like developing a cocaine habit while in an emotionally abusive relationship. Oprah never pretended to be perfect or to have all of the answers. She simply invited us on a journey.

Instead of exhausting your energy on staged perfection, look for opportunities to invite your audience on a journey so that everyone can be better together.

ARE YOU READY TO OWN THE POWER OF YOUR PLATFORM?

Technology has gifted ordinary people with the unprecedented ability to make a difference in the world. If you have an overwhelming desire to reach people with your message, you don't have to be wealthy, a supermodel or a Mensa-certified genius. All it takes is clarity and commitment.

If you're ready to grow your purpose-driven platform, a great place to start is figuring out your personal brand personality. Take my quiz at **Quiz.PlatformforPurpose.com**

PUT IT INTO PRACTICE
Growing Your Impact

Think of a person you don't know personally who has made a positive impact in your life by sharing their knowledge, wisdom or experiences. How did they reach you? What did you learn from them?

_____

_____

_____

What problem could you help people to solve with your knowledge, wisdom or experiences?

_____

_____

_____

How could their lives be better because of you?

_____

_____

_____

What stands in the way of making this a reality?

_____

_____

_____

Download exercise from the "Resources for Readers" section, password "Reader" at PlatformforPurposeBook.com.

ON PURPOSE / **12** Strategies to Reclaim Your Power and Change Your Life

Learn About
Ita Udo-Ema

Ita has been creating digital media for the past fifteen years. With a degree in computer animation from the Art Institute of Phoenix, Ita has co-produced three independent feature-length films, two network affiliate television programs, and published over 200 online videos.

In 2005, Ita founded the media studio, View from Above Entertainment, and works as an above-the-line video producer.

Connect with Ita Udo-Ema
Website: ViewfromAbove.net
Email: ita@viewfromabove.net

Chapter Eleven

Harnessing the Power of Storytelling

by Ita Udo-Ema

You might be too young to remember this, but when I was a kid, I loved Saturday morning cartoons. It was almost my religion. I watched all of the 80s classics: GI Joe, He-Man, ThunderCats, and most importantly, Transformers.

I loved Transformers. I still love these alien robots that transform into vehicles and protect the universe from their evil counterparts. I loved Transformers so much that my parents knew that come Christmas, if there wasn't a Transformer under the tree, we were gonna have problems.

Let me tell you about one Christmas in particular. But first, a little background. I was the kid that had a knack for finding the hiding place for his Christmas presents. There was no closet or cubby I wouldn't crawl through. I was the mighty hunter. No stone would be left unturned until I tracked down my prey. When I eventually found my prize, I was bold enough to think that I could meticulously and secretly open my gifts without getting caught. I would surgically peel back the tape and bask in the glory of the blueprints, instructions, and the catalog on new toys coming soon.

This Christmas morning started in a pretty typical fashion.

It's 5 am, so I spring out of bed and sprint to the living room in socked feet. My feet slid across the cool white-tiled floor as if I was the main character in a holiday version of the movie Risky Business.

Right there in front of the shimmering tree, illuminated in the glow of the Christmas lights, sat a green and red present with my name on it. I conducted my "investigation" days before, so I knew exactly what was waiting for me underneath that decorative wrap. I knew this was "Six Shot," a robot villain called a "Decepticon" that had six different transformations. It was the hottest new model out that year and I had to have it. I could hardly contain my excitement.

I waited with bated breath for my oldest brother to FINALLY get up. You see, he is 8 years older than me and an 18-year-old doesn't have the same sense of urgency as a 10-year-old when it comes to the crucial work of opening presents on Christmas morning.

When he finally joined us, I made a beeline for Six Shot. I stripped away the wrapping paper like a buzzsaw and there it was in its purple, green, and gray glory. Six Shot was mine.

I opened up the box and... it was empty. My heart sank.

Can you imagine how I felt? Can you picture that moment? Good. That's called narrative transportation.

At this point, I feel I owe you an apology. You probably feel like we took a hard left turn out of nowhere. We did. The title of this chapter is Story Crafting and I could think of no better way to demonstrate the effect stories can have by pulling you out of one, albeit abruptly. I promise I will make it up to you. In the following pages, I want to:

- Share what a story is, along with how and why it's effective marketing.
- Show you practically how to use your story to connect with your ideal clients and customers in your business.

Storytelling has become a hot topic in recent years. For the better part of two decades, I have been studying the art and science for storytelling, so it is funny and a little frustrating to hear it described as this fresh new thing.

> **Storytelling is built into our very nature. But that doesn't mean it comes naturally.**

In truth, the power of storytelling has always been around. It is a method that we rely on. Going back to the day of cave drawings, stories are the way we have always communicated.

There are a number of popular storytelling frameworks. All of the modern storytelling frameworks that you hear about today trace back to the work of Aristotle. I am here to tell you that we do not tell stories based on a specific model. We created these models to explain how we tell stories.

Storytelling is built into our very nature. But that doesn't mean it comes naturally. Let me tell you about my friend Helen.

STRUCTURING YOUR STORY FOR IMPACT

Helen is a wellness coach. She has a master's degree in nutrition. She is brilliant. She is bright. She is bubbly. And Helen cannot tell a story to save her life. She always starts off the same way. She is excited and anxious to share a story about a conversation she had or an event she just went to. She starts by setting the stage but then the threads start to unravel. She jumps back three days in the story. Then she remembers a detail from her high school experience, which becomes a segue into a conversation she had with her sister. And it's not uncommon to hear an "anyway, what was I saying?" thrown in for good measure.

Does this sound familiar? We all know a "Helen." If you don't, well, you might need to look in the mirror.

Helen's challenge isn't that she doesn't know her story. The problem is that she doesn't know how to structure it in a way that makes the most impact. To be a better and more persuasive communicator, learning to craft an effective story is a must.

HOW TO CRAFT A BETTER STORY

There are scores of books and research addressing the many facets of storytelling. It would be impossible to distill everything into a few thousand words. My goal in this chapter is to highlight some of the pitfalls to watch out for and ultimately help you craft a better story.

1. **Embrace Your Role as a Storyteller**
   Most of us have been acquainted with stories since childhood but allow me to share my favorite definition of "story":

   "The retelling of events, real or imagined, from a singular point of view."

   The first thing I want you to think about — the thing to embrace — is that you are the storyteller. You get to decide what to include. You get to decide what is relevant. A story is not merely, or necessarily, a recitation of fact. As the storyteller, you decide what to include and equally important, what to leave out.

One day Helen came to me for some help. She wanted to refine her sales pitch using story. In particular, she wanted to communicate her experience working with clients to help them lose weight. I thought this would be a great opportunity to walk her through my process.

"Great." I said, "I would be happy to coach you in story crafting."

She replied, "So where do we start?"

> "Begin at the beginning," the King said, very gravely, "and go on till you come to the end: then stop."
>
> Lewis Carroll, Alice in Wonderland

2. Begin at the Beginning

   A bit over-simplified, but Lewis Carol had a point. I told Helen that the place to start is with the acknowledgment that stories have a very specific structure. Stories have a beginning, a middle, and an end.

   I know that might seem self-evident. I reminded her of that pitfall she runs into, the reason her story goes ricocheting all over the place is that she forgets this simple tenant. When you are telling a story, you are taking your audience on a journey. Each step along that journey is a "beat."

3. **Define the "Beats" of Your Story**
   Beats are the core building blocks of a story. They are the individual elements that make up your story. The beats you choose to use and how you put them together will define the impact of your story. As I mentioned in the previous step, we have to start at the beginning, so the first beat in your story should set up the world or context of your story. In Helen's case, I told her to set the stage by sharing who she is and how she arrived at her current level of expertise.

   "There is so much," she replied.

   Perhaps — like Helen — you're wondering if you need to share every detail with your audience. Your listeners don't need to hear everything; just what is relevant to the promise or solution you're offering in sharing your story. The mistake we all frequently make is we forget that a story is a snapshot in time. We don't have one story. We have many and they have different facets and angles.

   What happens is that we want to share it all. We don't want to leave any parts out, but effective storytelling isn't about telling "all the parts." It's about telling the right parts, in the right order. Let's revisit the "beats" of Helen's story:

   Who are you?

   "My name is Helen Hayes."

   And what do you do?

   "I am a wellness coach."

   Great! And how did you get here?

   With any story, you want to guide your audience along a path. To do so, you want to choose beats along that path. Nothing else. You want "causality." You want one beat to lead to the next and the next.

DISCOVERING YOUR BEATS WITH "THE RULE OF THREES"

The late Hollywood film editor Norman Hollyn coined the phrase "The Rule of Threes." The "Rule of Threes" states that every scene is informed by the scene that came before it. In turn, each scene informs the one that follows it. Likewise, every beat of your story should be informed by the beat that came before it and informs the one that comes after it.

After setting the stage with beat one, you'll want to move on to the next beat, which is often referred to at the inciting incident or the conflict. It is the "why" of your story. It sets the story in motion. I drew out the inciting incident of Helen's story with a simple question:

"Helen, why did you become a wellness coach?"

"In my studies, I found that people were relying on fads and diets when what they really needed to do was take a broader look at their lifestyle."

Seeing her people fail to hit their weight loss goals with fad-diets triggered Helen to take action, specifically by coaching others to weight loss success by creating healthier habits and routines. Can you see how this beat builds upon the first?

The next 3-5 beats are the journey. These are the events that took place along the path. Since Helen wanted to focus on how she helped clients I ask the obvious question: "Helen, how do you help your clients?"

She replied that she would sit down with them, ask some guided questions, and then put together a plan. I pressed her to "zoom in." I asked for details. By giving specific details you build authenticity within your story.

"Helen, what are the guided questions?"

She first questions her clients about their dietary goals. Then she asks about their family history with regards to high blood pressure and diabetes and their daily routine. Based on her client's answers, among others, she creates a meal schedule.

But what happens when Helen's clients struggle to execute their carefully crafted weight loss plan?

EMBRACE THE FALL

While it'd be great for business if every client experience went off without a hitch, we all know that things sometimes go wrong. The same is true in any dynamic story. There is rising action and falling action. No one ever cheered a story where the hero was good and just kept getting better and better. The hero always experiences a "fall." It's the experience of falling and getting back up that connects with the protagonist. Let's see how this plays out for Helen.

"Helen what do you do when things go wrong?"

"What do you mean?"

"What do you do when the plan goes wrong?"

"I don't want to talk about that. It's so negative."

"Of course, you do," I said.

"Well, I do offer follow-up consultations in case they have trouble sticking to the meal plan."

"That's perfect!" I exclaim. "Now, all that's left is to put it all together. Here's your story, Helen:

'My name is Helen Hayes and I'm a wellness coach. In

my 15 years studying nutrition and fitness, I found that people were relying too much on fads and quick-fix diets when what they really needed to do was take a broader look at their lifestyle. I sit down with my clients and ask them about their family history with regards to high blood pressure and diabetes. I ask my clients about their daily routines. Based on these answers, among others, I create a meal schedule for my clients. And if they fall off the wagon — which happens to the best of us — I offer follow-up coaching and support.'"

NARRATIVE TRANSPORTATION

I began our time together by telling you a story about my childhood to demonstrate a principle called "narrative transportation." So... what is narrative transportation? It's one of the key elements of storytelling. It's why storytelling is so powerful.

Have you ever been lost in a story? It's that experience when you are on the edge of your seat completely invested in the characters and plot—in anxious anticipation over what will happen next. I'll leave you with one final example of narrative transportation before I go.

Imagine you're sitting in bed. It's just after 10 p.m. The light is low and you are reading the latest Stephen King thriller. The skeptical sheriff that's been tracking down a series of mysterious disappearances has been led to the old house at the end of town. As he approaches the large oak doors, the wind whistles through the trees. He draws the door open and BAM! I don't know...a thing happens and you physically jump in your seat.

Now I don't pretend to be anywhere near the writer Stephen King is but, hopefully, you get the idea. Even though you are perfectly safe at home in your bed, the story has pulled you into that bone-chilling moment within the story. Imagine this power being put to work in your brand messaging. Can you see how using story crafting can create a connection with your audience and create real urgency that motivates them to take action?

Narrative transportation is the way we bypass the logic and reason centers of the brain. It's how we persuade. Studies have shown that when a person is transported into a story, they are more likely to accept the information that they are being presented with. Moreover, that information or belief resonates in their subconscious long after the story has been told.

In research from a 2000 study on the role of transportation in the persuasiveness of public narrative, the authors state,

"To the extent that individuals are absorbed into a story or transported into a narrative world, they may show effects of the story on their real-world beliefs." *(Brock/Green)*

By carefully and deliberately choosing your story's beats, you'll foster engagement with your audience. When you zoom in and share specific details, your brand breeds authenticity. Finally, in your messaging, acknowledge that everyone falls sometimes. Embrace that falling action, then reinforce that strong connection by sharing the solution you're prepared to provide to help your hero (the client) rise again. These are the keys to crafting a message that is both compelling and meaningful.

I have done my best to share some of the secrets of storytelling in this chapter. Throughout the process, it's felt a bit like explaining how a magic trick works. If you feel a bit like Helen and you'd like personal coaching to help to craft your story, I would like to invite you to contact me. Let's set up a call and talk "story." You can connect with at **http://www2.ViewFromAbove.net/consultation.**

One last thing: In case you were wondering, at the end of that Christmas, after all the presents had been unwrapped, my parents chuckled with glee. My mom, in her fuzzy blue housecoat, reached behind the couch and pulled out Six-

Shot. I think that was the second-best Christmas I ever had.

The first best Christmas? Well, that's a different story.

PUT IT INTO PRACTICE
3 Brand Story Recipes

Now that you've seen how impactful narrative transportation can be in your business, let's get you crafting your own brand stories with these three simple recipes.

Recipe #1: The Refined Sales Pitch

Let's begin with the obvious, low-hanging fruit here by refining your sales pitch, as Helen and I did. Define your story's beats by answering the questions below. Feel free to refer back to Helen's example within my chapter if you get stuck.

Set the Stage - Who is your ideal client? What is their life like? What is their current reality?

_____

_____

_____

Inciting Conflict - What has happened in life that triggered an immediate need to change?

_____

_____

_____

Embrace the Fall - What struggles are they facing as they go through this change?

_____

_____

_____

Call to Action - What should your ideal audience member do right now to receive your solution?

___

___

___

Recipe #2: The Nurture Post (or Email)

Here's where things get a little spicier for your biz using story crafting. A nurture post or email aims to address an objection your audience member may have to a product you intend to pitch to them in the near future.

With that objection in mind, craft a story that debunks any false belief that could potentially hold your audience back from buying or demonstrates how failing to apply your expertise could potentially be more costly. Be sure to do this authentically.

Set the Stage - What objection could potentially hold your audience back from changing their situation? What loss or pain do they hope to avoid by clinging to that objection?

___

___

___

Inciting Conflict - Hook them with a story or illustrate how this objection is actually causing them pain by keeping them stuck. Ask, if the worst-case scenario they imagine is truly as grave as it seems.

___

___

___

ON PURPOSE / **12** Strategies to Reclaim Your Power and Change Your Life

Embrace the Fall - Acknowledging that scenario "could" be true, introduce the growth that could take place if they let go of that objection. What could they gain in exchange?

_____

_____

_____

Call to Action - What should your ideal audience member do right now to receive your solution?

_____

_____

_____

Recipe #3: The Trust-Building Tutorial (Works for posts and videos)

Nothing builds your ideal audience's trust faster than your proven ability to get them a quick win. Help your audience get one step closer to achieving their goal with a simple, instructional post or video.

Set the Stage - What does your audience want to achieve? Build anticipation by zooming in on the "why" that motivates them.

_____

_____

_____

Inciting Conflict - If possible, demonstrate why alternatives to the solution you're offering are less effective. Then share your improved process to achieve their goal.

_____
_____
_____

Embrace the Fall - Are there any tips or hacks your audience can implement if they encounter problems along the way?

_____
_____
_____

Call to Action - Remind your audience how you helped them move one step closer to their goal. Then invite them to walk through your entire process with your paid product or service.

_____
_____
_____

Learn About
Sarah R. Adams

Sarah R. Adams is an award-winning multimedia producer, freelance reporter, writer, and educator with over 20 years of professional experience in broadcasting and higher education. She has extensive experience as a television producer, on-air personality and host, radio news reporter, and author. Adams is also an experienced managing non-profit public relations and promotions, as well as providing media consulting services.

Adams currently teaches multimedia writing, media on-air performance, and media criticism courses for Central Michigan University's School of Broadcast and Cinematic Arts.

Connect with Sarah R. Adams
Email: sarah.r.adams246@gmail.com

Chapter Twelve

The Importance of Being You

by Sarah R. Adams

It seems that my entire life I've been trying to find myself, and I know I'm not alone in feeling this way. A quick Google search reveals a whopping 14,240,000,000 results for the phrase "How do I find out who I am?" That's a lot of people hungry for answers! The search results lead to self-help books, online programs, life coaches, articles, news stories — all trying to help frantic searchers discover the heart of who they truly are.

It's easy to lose track of who you are, especially when you've worked in television and radio for a long time like I did. But thanks to Rick, my first boss after college, I didn't fall prey to that confusion. Early in my career as a media professional, Rick shared an Oscar Wilde quote with me that I'll never forget: "Be yourself; everyone else is already taken." That moment truly changed my life.

Perhaps you can relate to spending years trying to find your identity and fit in with those around you? As a child, I struggled with the camera-ready faces and body types I saw in my favorite TV shows. I felt like glasses, freckles, and my untamable, thick and curly red hair made me an anomaly in a sea of sleek blondes and brunettes during my middle school years. My search for identity continued to unfold as time marched on. I waffled between labels such as "the pastor's kid," "awkward bookworm," and "straight-A student." Then I settled into my phase as the gradually-emboldened community theater performer and singer, public speaker, and local pageant queen.

In college and the years beyond, I began to adopt my professional identity: Radio personality, news reporter, television host, documentary producer, then public relations and promotions planner. Deep down, I wished for perfect "anchor hair" and high cheekbones; I longed to look like the willowy Disney princesses of my childhood or the other people in my chosen profession. I longed to have the unattainable polish that peers around me seemed to magically find without effort. Looking back, I can see that I wanted to be someone I had created in my mind. Someone who wasn't me.

And then came that Oscar Wilde quote from Rick as I began my career with Public Television: "Be yourself; everyone else is already taken." The more I thought about the words, the more I realized that I had something valuable to contribute to the world that no one else could... simply by being myself. It profoundly changed how I viewed myself, and it profoundly changed how I viewed my career.

These days, I'm a professor of media writing and on-air performance classes at a university, essentially teaching my students how to do what I used to do in the media industry. As I watch these learners grow over the semesters, I often think back to that quote my mentor shared with me. Like Rick, I actively seek to instill that concept of being yourself into the students I now teach.

I've realized that the best instruction I give my students doesn't come from a textbook. Instead, it comes from the advice that people like Rick and others have infused in me over the years, as well as the lessons learned about becoming what we in the media business call "talent" (that's the person in front of the camera or microphone). You just might be surprised by how much you can learn about life by prepping to put yourself in an on-air performance situation!

I remind my students all of the time that:

1. **You have got to be yourself.**
   That Oscar Wilde quote I mentioned before has become the mantra in the classes I teach about on-air performance. I tell my students that you have to remember that viewers can spot a phony a mile away. So, when the lights and cameras go on, you really have to simply be yourself. Now this can be scary and intimidating — being the true, unedited version of ourselves.

   Whether it's in front of a camera lens, or being in a new career or relationship in our personal life, showing up authentically is like inviting people to peer into the window of our souls. But keep in mind that this transparency is worth it in the long run. Others need to know what you have to offer. The more you practice simply being yourself, you'll find it's easier to stay calm and grounded and accomplish the goals you want to achieve — just like my on-air performance students do when it's time to "go live."

2. **But be the BEST version of yourself.**
   I tell my students that polishing their on-air performance is not the same as being a fake version of themselves. Being the best version of yourself doesn't mean changing who you are. Instead, it means playing up your strengths and downplaying your weaknesses (Or, as I like to call them with my students, your "work-ons"). Usually my students are way tougher on themselves than I ever would be when we watch a recording of their projects. So, I encourage them to notice their strengths and focus on those...all the while

encouraging them to take inventory of things that could be a distraction so they can figure out how to downplay them.

A part of this honest evaluation is also knowing your worth. Think of this analogy: Some violins sell for under $30; others go for as much as $13,000. That's not even counting the instruments that are famous throughout history because they were created by a master craftsman. And aren't you more valuable than a violin or other musical instrument? Know your worth and exercise that knowledge by taking care of yourself. This self-care takes place when you work to preserve your inner beauty and functionality.

> **YOU are important, what you have to say is important, and people need the information you have to offer.**

Taking care of yourself through hydration, rest, nutrition, and mental health ensures that your instrument, your body, will play well for you. On-air performance is about using your whole body to convey the message you want to send into the camera or microphone, and I like to think that's a great metaphor for life: when you're taking care of you, your whole self will reflect the best you.

3. **Then, be confident in you.**
   I always tell my students it's about what they DO with the fear and adrenaline that starts to race as they step in front of a camera or microphone. For them, it's about calming the fears they have about "going live," reading off of a teleprompter under bright studio lights, or thinking on their feet in the middle of a breaking news situation. But I'll tell you the same thing I tell them: The

people around you only know you're nervous and unsure if you let them know you're nervous and unsure... so be bold!

Another secret I tell my students is that successfully being in front of a camera or microphone is 85% confidence. One key to increasing your confidence is realizing that what you have to say is important. Go into each situation with that mindset. YOU are important, what you have to say is important, and people need the information you have to offer. You'll be amazed at what a confidence boost that is! And keep in mind: The more you practice this mindset, the more confident you'll become.

If you're reading this book, I'm sure that you've decided to 'up your game,' professionally or personally...or maybe even both. Perhaps you're an expert in your field with great information to share on bigger platforms. Maybe you want to become braver by putting yourself out there and trying new opportunities. Maybe you're even intrigued by the coaching I offer my students and professionals like you when it comes to putting yourself in front of a camera and speaking with confidence about what you have to offer the world on various platforms. Maybe you're simply seeking the answer to that age-old question that's always in the back of my mind: Just who am I, and what is my purpose?

I believe discovering ourselves is a process that is ongoing. Just like my students practicing being in front of a camera or microphone in preparation for their media careers, every day you'll learn something new. Sometimes you'll feel energized and on top of your game. Other days, you'll cringe as you finish the day wrapped up in a blanket trying not to think about everything that transpired. But remember: Whether you are performing in front of a camera or simply working on your personal or professional self, you have to be you. You have to be your best you, all the while remembering that your best is going to look just a little bit different every day. So, as the process of being your BEST you unfolds, be confident and enjoy the ride. And don't be afraid to reach out for a little help along the way.

*Visit **PlatformforPurpose.com** for upcoming on-air performance training with Sarah R. Adams designed for experts and thought leaders.*

PUT IT INTO PRACTICE
Rediscovering YOU 3-Day Challenge

Day One
Gain new insights about your personality by taking the Enneagram or CliftonStrengths personality test. (Optional: Invite a friend or coworker to do the same and compare results.) You'll be amazed at how coming to understand yourself (and others) will help you communicate your needs, re-energize yourself, and establish boundaries in every area of your life.

Day Two
Design a one-day retreat to reconnect with yourself. The goal here isn't to create a retreat you can afford or take immediately, but to allow yourself to dream about your getaway without limitations. Details such as the location, activities, and the community (or isolation) where you find refreshment, speak to what energizes you. These details are essential to keeping your physical, emotional, and mental cup full.

Day Three
I hope you didn't think I'd let you go without allowing you an opportunity to show up in front of the camera! Use your smartphone or camera to record yourself giving a brief tutorial for family and friends. Don't get hung up choosing your topic. You can share an instructional video on something as simple and fun as a dance move that was popular when you were growing up. Or, get practical with a technical tutorial or prepare your favorite recipe. After you've finished, take the time to watch yourself, share it with at least one loved one, and together, celebrate how your personality shines through.

Download exercise from the "Resources for Readers" section, password "Reader" at PlatformforPurposeBook.com.

Final Thoughts

by Isha Cogborn

Whether you jumped around or read the book from cover to cover, I congratulate you for making it here. If you didn't take the time to do so initially, do yourself a favor and complete the exercises at the end of the chapters that resonate with where you are right now. We often hear the phrase, "knowledge is power", but in reality, applied knowledge is power.

To download the action guide independently, visit **PlatformforPurposeBook.com** and enter the code **READER**. Consider purchasing a book for a friend and holding each other accountable to the strategies outlined. I also encourage you to reach out to the authors. They are all equipped to help you get to your next level, which is why they were selected to be a part of this book.

Life isn't easy and it isn't always fair, but it can still be good when you make a decision to push through the obstacles and take action to live purposefully. My prayer is that you picked up a nugget or two from this book that will help you along the journey.

I also encourage you to build or connect to a community of like-minded people who want more than the status quo.

We aren't meant to do life alone. Don't let the fact that people may have let you down in the past keep you isolated from the help you need to reach your goals.

The world is full of people with passions they never pursued. Great ideas they never followed up on. Incredible visions they never even uttered. Don't let that be you! If you have a dream in your heart that won't go away, it's there for a reason. You owe it to yourself and the people who will benefit from what you have to offer to pursue it.

To access additional personal and professional development resources, visit **EpiphanyInstitute.com**

To join a mastermind community focused on helping entrepreneurs overcome the fear, overwhelm and isolation of starting and growing your business, visit **StartupLifeSupport.com**.

If you're a expert, thought leader, coach or consultant who wants to make a bigger impact with your knowledge or by creating platforms that change the world, visit **PlatformforPurpose.com**.

NOTES

Chapter 3: How to Fight Fear and Build Authentic Confidence

1. Francesco Drago, "Self-Esteem and Earnings," IZA Discussion Paper. No. 3577, Self- Esteem and Earnings by Francesco Drago :: SSRN.

Chapter 7: Ten Ways to Live a More Natural Life Everyday

1. Nicola Slawson, "Regularly Using Bleach Leads to Higher Risk of Fatal Lung Disease," The Guardian, Accessed February 10, 2020, https://www.theguardian.com/uk-news/2017/sep/11/regularly-using-bleach-linked-to-higher-risk-of-fatal-lung-disease.

2. Janice Stewart, "Hydrogen Peroxide + Vinegar, a Disinfecting Duo?" Cleaning Business Today, Accessed January 30, 2020, https://cleaningbusinesstoday.com/blog/hydrogen-peroxide-vinegar-a-disinfecting-duo/.

3. Joseph Mercola, "How Artificial Sweeteners Confuse Your Body into Storing Fat and Inducing Diabetes," Mercola, Accessed February 10, 2020, https://articles.mercola.com/sites/articles/archive/2014/12/23/artificial-sweeteners-confuse-body.aspx#.

4. Adana AM Llanos, et al.,"Hair product use and breast cancer risk among African American and White women," Carcinogenesis, Volume 38, Issue 9, September 2017, 883–892, https://doi.org/10.1093/carcin/bgx060.

5. Daily Health Post Editorial, "This is What Happens 10 Hours After Putting on Nail Polish," Daily Health Post, April 4, 2019, https://dailyhealthpost.com/toxic-nail-polish-and-natural-alternatives/.

6. Katie Wells, "Is EMF Exposure Really a Big Deal?" WellnessMama, Updated January 5, 2020, https://wellnessmama.com/129645/emf-exposure/.

7. Laughter cite Mayo Clinic Staff, "Stress Relief from Laughter? It's No Joke!" Mayo Clinic, April 5, 2019, https://www.mayoclinic.org/healthy-lifestyle/stress-management/in-depth/stress-relief/art-20044456.

8. Annie Price, "9 Awesome Health Benefits of Dark Chocolate," Dr. Axe. November 28, 2019, https://draxe.com/nutrition/benefits-of-dark-chocolate/.

Chapter 12: Story Crafting in Your Business

1. Patrick Moreau, "The 4 Pillars of Story," Business 2 Community, https://www.business2community.com/marketing/the-4-pillars-of-story-01333266.

2. Melanie C. Green and Timothy C. Brock, "The Role of Transportation in the Persuasiveness of Public Narrative," PubMed, https://www.researchgate.net/publication/12248972_The_Role_of_Transportation_in_the_Persuasiveness_of_Public_Narrative.

Made in the USA
Columbia, SC
27 September 2024

42514101R10089